# St Lucia

Footprint

Sarah Cameron

# Contents

## Listings

# About the author

After a degree in Latin American Studies Sarah Cameron has been travelling and writing on the continent ever since, both as an economist and as an author for Footprint Handbooks. Initially moonlighting for the South American Handbook while working for a British bank, in 1990 she parted company with the world of finance and has been contributing to the expansion of Footprint titles ever since. Sarah now concentrates solely on the Caribbean and is the author of Footprint Caribbean Islands as well as individual island titles such as Cuba, the Dominican Republic, Barbados, St Lucia, Antigua and the Leeward Islands. When she is not travelling around the Caribbean sampling beaches and rum cocktails, she retreats to her 17th-century farmhouse in rural Suffolk.

# Acknowledgements

Sarah Cameron is most grateful to Maria Grech, long-time resident in St Lucia and correspondent for Footprint Caribbean Islands, for her help in checking and updating information for this new book and generally keeping an eye on things on the island. Thanks also go to Patricia Charlery at the St Lucia Tourist Board in London and Maria Hunte in Castries for their help in organizing accommodation and transport during Sarah's research trip to St Lucia. Sarah is indebted to Colette McDermott, of Cara Hotels, for fun, friendship, hospitality, entertainment and cricket, and to Tony Thorne, of Wilderness Explorers for helping her back up the steps of the Enbas Saut Trail and great companionship.

Schoolgirls dressed in neat blue uniforms, with their hair pulled back into tight braids, chatter on their way to school. Ripe mangoes squashed on the road, too many to eat, ferment in the heat. Cinnamon and nutmeg waft up from the market and the frying of fish fills the Friday night air. A blast of steel pan music assails you from a tourist hotel and parrots call from deep in the emerald rainforest. The heady perfume of flowers at Mamiku Gardens contrasts with the stench of sulphur at the Soufrière volcano. Solid stone fortresses highlight the vulnerabilities of timber homes. Turtles drag themselves onto the deserted golden beaches on the east coast just as fishermen haul their brightly coloured fishing boats onto the dark volcanic sand of the southwest.

From the green of the breadfruit to the blue of the sea via a hand of yellow bananas and a scarlet ginger lily, the colours of St Lucia provide a sumptuous feast for all the senses.

## Culture vultures

St Lucia (pronounced 'Loosha') has a rich cultural heritage from the alternating French and British colonial powers and the African slaves brought in to work their plantations. This particular Caribbean pot of races and cultures has produced a language known as *Kwéyòl*, spoken by most St Lucians. On the island you will find French architecture, French place-names, Creole cuisine and Roman Catholicism, while the official language is English, cars drive on the left and cricket is the most popular sport. Some of the finest writers and artists in the region come from St Lucia: magnificent murals adorn churches in country parishes; galleries exhibit the work of the many local painters and sculptors who find inspiration in their surroundings; and the island has produced two Nobel prize winners, one for Economics, the other for Literature - the highest per capita number of Nobel Laureates ever, anywhere.

## A breath of fresh air

While you may want to laze on the beach or lie in a hammock and gaze on the majesty of the Pitons, there is much in St Lucia to tempt you away from soporific delights. The turquoise sea offers exciting sailing, scuba diving, deep-sea fishing, whale watching or just some gentle snorkelling. Athletic types can try their hand at windsurfing or even kiteboarding. On land, you can test your legs and lungs by biking or hiking up mountains, along river beds and through forests - the interior is outstandingly beautiful and forest reserves protect watersheds as well as the St Lucian parrot and other wildlife. Manicured greens can be found on the golf course, the cricket pitch or the tennis court. You may then need a massage but that too is available at a spa. Sightseeing opportunities include the capital, Castries, colonial fortifications and plantation tours. To round off your day you can enjoy a high standard of cooking in the restaurants, rums in the bars, street parties for local seafood, fish fries and 'jump-ups' and the beat of soca, zouk or reggae late into the night in the clubs and discos of Rodney Bay.

# At a glance

## Castries

The capital city lies on one of the Caribbean's most beautiful natural harbours and was quickly chosen by Europeans in the 16th century as the perfect place to set up base. Since then the port has always been busy handling cargo, war ships and now cruise ships. The city sprawls over steep hillsides, offering picturesque sea views for business and government offices as well as its residents. Several town fires have destroyed many of the oldest buildings, now replaced with modern concrete blocks, but the setting outweighs the lack of architectural distinction. A morning spent wandering around the market, the Roman Catholic cathedral and Derek Walcott Square will uncover the charms of the old city with its French style of architecture, while a trip up the Morne will reveal the strategic importance of the harbour, a safe haven for shipping for centuries.

## North to Rodney Bay and Gros Islet

Most visitors stay in this area, where there are good beaches, hotels, restaurants, nightlife, sporting facilities and the marina. This is the place to come for an action-packed beach holiday, whether you want to be self-catering, go all-inclusive or find a comfortable mid-range hotel where you can do your own thing. Rodney Bay is the centre of most activities, with a large marina offering services to independent yachtsmen, charter fleets and day trippers. The village area is packed with small hotels, restaurants and bars offering a variety of cuisine and entertainment all day and well into the night. Away from the main tourist drag, you can get a feel for traditional St Lucian village life in Gros Islet, where there are small, family-run restaurants serving local food on the main street and the sea front. The atmosphere changes on a Friday night, however, when the whole place becomes a vibrant street party with barbecue stalls, rum shops and loud music, known as a 'jump-up'.

A causeway leads out to Pigeon Island, a former military outpost and covered in ruins of military installations from the days when the British Navy ruled the waves. Fascinating for a day of historical exploration, it is also the site of many of the concerts held during the annual Jazz Festival, one of the biggest events of its kind in the region and not to be missed by music lovers. Inland and up in the hills away from the bustle of the beach resorts is the island's only zoo, containing a small collection of endangered St Lucian creatures. It is also the headquarters for the Forestry Department, who control the Forest Reserves and most of the hiking trails around the island.

## The north and northeast coasts

The north is the driest part of the island, where the vegetation is more scrub and cactus than the lush rainforest found in the south. A certain amount of tourist development has taken place here, with a golf course and luxury villas, but it is a quiet area. The northeast coast beaches are wild and untamed, battered by the Atlantic and are great for hiking and beachcombing but most are not for swimming.

## East coast to Vieux Fort

The dramatic Atlantic coast is dotted with fishing villages which grew at the mouths of rivers for fresh water supply. Dennery is a good place to go for fish fry at weekends and is on an exceptionally scenic stretch of coastline with groins and sea walls protecting the fishing harbour as well as islets and cliffs. Much of the coast is ecologically diverse and there are several protected zones. At Praslin the Eastern Nature Trail runs between the road and the sea. Fregate Island is a Heritage Site, while Mamiku Gardens offer a fantastic display of tropical blooms in a historical setting. Everywhere along the road you will see sheds for washing and packing bananas, a reminder of the economic mainstay of the island's farmers. Many of the rainforest walks can be accessed from this side for birdwatching and hiking. The Des Cartiers trail links up with trails starting on the other side of the island. Further south along the coast you come to Savannes Bay, where they farm sea moss, before you get to Anse de Sables and Vieux Fort at the southern tip, watched over by the lighthouse on Cap Moule à Chique, said to be the second highest in the world. You can get a tremendous view from the top, looking up the island to Morne Gimie and the Pitons. At Pointe Sable National Park is the southern office of the St Lucia National Trust and access to the Maria Islands. The windswept sandy beach is almost deserted as there is currently no hotel, although the water is usually dotted with the colourful sails of windsurfers and kiteboarders, flitting about like butterflies. Vieux Fort is a business town, with a duty free zone and the international airport.

## West coast to Soufrière and the Pitons

Stunning mountain scenery and dozens of pretty bays make this the most beautiful part of the island. Marigot Bay is one of the prettiest yacht harbours in the Caribbean and has been used several times in film and television. In the neighbourhood of the Pitons, recently declared a World Heritage Site, the scenery has an element of grandeur. The highest peak is Morne Gimie but the most spectacular are Gros Piton and Petit Piton, old volcanic, forest-clad plugs rising sheer out of the sea near the town of Soufrière. Close by is one of the world's most accessible volcanoes with *soufrières*: vents in the volcano which exude sulphurous vapours. The mountains are intersected by numerous short rivers which in places debouch into broad, fertile and well-cultivated valleys. Bananas, cocoa and coffee are all grown here, as well as fruit and vegetables for domestic consumption, often in small patches clinging to steep hillsides. The rainforest is green and lush and home to numerous indigenous birds, such as the endangered St Lucia parrot, whose numbers are steadily increasing thanks to conservation efforts.

# Trip planner

At any time of year you can get plenty of hot sunshine, but don't expect it to be dry all day every day. The dry season is roughly from January to May with showers to keep things green. The rainy season should start in June lasting almost to the end of the year with occasional hurricanes. However, climate changes have had an effect on rainfall and any distinctions between dry and wet seasons are now blurred. Tropical storms are most likely to occur in September to November and can cause flooding and mudslides. The north of the island is less prone to rain than the south, but you can expect showers at any time of year, with more falling in the mountains than on the coast. The mean annual temperature is about 26°C, but the northeast trade winds are a cooling influence.

You can time your visit to coincide with Carnival in July when you can join in with the festivities, including colourful parades and pageants, music and competitions. The greatest influx of visitors is usually for the annual Jazz Festival in May, when open-air concerts by internationally renowned artists are held around the island. Other events to consider are Test Matches, when cricket fans travel to support their team, or the arrival of the Atlantic Rally for Cruisers in the first week of December, when Rodney Bay fills with yachts and their crew, hell-bent on enjoying themselves on terra firma.

## A weekend

If you only have a couple of days to spare, you should try and take in Friday evening activities, with the fish fry at Anse La Raye or the jump-up at Gros Islet. Both are street parties where the food and booze are in abundance and having a good time is guaranteed. Rodney Bay is probably the best area to base yourself for a weekend, with the beach, watersports, restaurants, bars and clubs all within walking distance. If you have the time, do a day trip to Soufrière and the Pitons; most excursions start from the marina or pick up at hotels in the area.

## A week or more

St Lucia is a small volcanic island just 27 miles long by 14 miles wide but, with a mountainous spine, if you don't want to be driving on mountain roads all the time, consider a two-centre holiday. You could divide your time between the activities of Rodney Bay and the peace of a country area with the forest at your doorstep. A walk in the rainforest is not to be missed: the views are spectacular, with majestic mountains, steep valleys and endless shades of green. An overnight tour to see the leatherback turtles laying their eggs on Grand Anse beach is a must as is a whale-watching trip. There are about 20 species of whales and dolphins in the waters around St Lucia.

If you have an unlimited budget, a few nights at the intimate Ladera Resort in Soufrière will allow you to unwind as you gaze upon the Pitons. Alternatively, Anse Chastanet offers the beach, diving and snorkelling in the marine park. Both these, and others which cost a little less such as The Still Plantation and Beach Resort, offer amazing views – hard to beat anywhere in the Caribbean. Guest houses in Soufrière provide simpler lodgings in the shadow of the Pitons. You can visit the sulphur springs, tour the south of the island and hike in Edmond Forest Reserve. If you are interested in birds, there are many endemic species, including the St Lucia parrot, rescued from near extinction. Try the Millet Trail, a little further north, as it takes in Roseau Dam and a fresh-water lake.

On the east coast, Mamiku Gardens will take hours of a keen gardener's time – allow more if your interest lies in archaeology. You can visit Fregate Island Nature Reserve, the East Coast Nature Trail and Savannes Bay all in a day but do allow a whole day just for the Maria Islands, so you can take advantage of the beach there before you return to Anse de Sables for beach bars, windsurfing and kiteboarding. The Des Cartiers Rainforest Trail takes two hours, but serious hikers can join up with other trails, crossing the island to the Edmond Forest Reserve. There are fewer places to stay on the east coast but they are worth trying and won't break the bank.

## Best

### Ten of the best

1 Anse La Raye Friday fish fry with the best seafood caught in local waters, p73.

2 A Test Match at Beausejour cricket ground, one of the best pitches in the West Indies, p153.

3 Dive in the marine park at Soufrière for a pristine underworld adventure, p78

4 Sail from Rodney Bay down the west coast for a view of the cliffs, forests and majestic Pitons, p28.

5 Turtle watching on Grand Anse, an overnight vigil of the leatherbacks hauling themselves up the sand to lay their eggs, p54.

6 Hike and birdwatch in the Edmond Forest, deep in the tropical nature reserve, p86

7 Take a boat trip to the Maria Islands to find the rare racer snake, colourful ground lizards and nesting birds, p67.

8 Explore Pigeon Island and its history of forts and battles in colonial days, p49.

9 Shop in Castries market for spices, fruit, cocoa sticks, coal pots and other souvenirs, p36

10 Kiteboarding or windsurfing at Anse de Sables where wind conditions are exciting but you won't get carried out to the ocean, p66.

Hiring a car is the best way of exploring the island, but remember that the mountain roads into the forests are very poor. A 4WD or high clearance is recommended. If you don't want to drive yourself, there are tours to anywhere you might want to go and guides can always be arranged. The Forestry Department and Heritage Tours are well placed to organize customized itineraries. Minibuses provide a reasonable public transport system but will not get you far off the beaten track.

# Contemporary St Lucia

Life on St Lucia might appear idyllic to visitors, but for the island's residents, living here is not entirely problem-free. Opportunities for education, employment and self-advancement are limited and St Lucia is no different from other Caribbean islands in this respect. After four centuries of French and British colonial rule, in 2004 St Lucia celebrated 25 years of independence as a democracy. But those 25 years have seen the island struggling to build a strong economy under difficult circumstances.

St Lucians see education as the key to progress and parents put huge emphasis on getting their children to school even if it means scrimping and saving for school books and uniforms. St Lucian children receive a solid, if slightly old-fashioned education based on the former British system, but once they leave school, their opportunities are limited. There are menial jobs in hotels and catering with their overtones of neo-colonialism and memories of masters and slaves, but few prospects, and this does sometimes lead to problems with disaffected youth and drugs. For those with good grades, university education has to be taken abroad, either at the University of the West Indies, with its campuses dotted around the larger islands, or further still, in the USA, Canada or Britain. Those that make the break often remain abroad afterwards, where jobs are more readily available, coming home for Christmas or family celebrations, or to retire, building luxury houses on Rodney Heights which they never could have afforded in the UK.

St Lucia's two political parties have their roots in the economic decline of the 1930s, a decade which saw strikes by coal handlers and sugar workers in demand of higher wages. Out of conflict, the seeds of a labour movement grew. Their militancy brought the formation of the first trade union which later developed into the first political party, the St Lucia Labour Party (SLP). Universal adult suffrage was introduced in 1951 and since that year elections have been held regularly, won either by the SLP or the United Workers Party (UWP). The SLP are currently governing the country and have been in power since 1997. Still holding on to a sizeable majority, over the last few years the party's crown has definitely slipped and the government of Dr. Kenneth Anthony is waning in popularity.

With only tourism and bananas to sustain jobs and income, neither party has managed to build a strong economy, independent of world events. Tourism is now the major employer and foreign exchange earner, and some 250,000 visitors stay on the island each year. However, this too is subject to the vagaries of the world economic and political situation and an event such as 9/11 can have serious repercussions on the fortunes of St Lucians.The bombing of the World Trade Center in 2001 knocked tourism for six and many hotels were forced to close for a while or sell up. Once the shock wore off and Americans started to travel again, things picked up and tourism in St Lucia is now booming, and several new hotels have opened in the last year or so.

The banana industry remains in crisis, however, since the trade wars of the 1980s and 1990s. St Lucia still has the largest banana crop in the Windward Islands, but production has slumped. Farmers have suffered because of low prices, storm damage and labour disputes and many have fallen by the wayside. Greater competition in the European banana market, particularly after EC unification in 1992, is leading to diversification away from bananas, but although there has been an attempt to promote cocoa this has not really been successful. Currently there is a move to promote heavier use of the banana locally as well as within the tourist industry – apparently St Lucians have the lowest consumption of bananas in the world! This may or may not be true but they certainly do not eat a lot of ripe bananas, preferring 'green figs' (unripe bananas) as a staple.

St Lucia's population of around 156,000 remains conscious of its colourful past. Archaeological discoveries of the Amerindians who lived on the island before the Europeans arrived are treated with respect by the people, if not by investors wanting to build hotels, and their customs have been preserved for posterity. It is still possible to see how St Lucia's previous inhabitants, now known as the Island Arawaks, made their houses, hunted, gathered and prepared their food. The French influence on the island is also notable, even though they were ejected nearly 200 hundred years ago, and people continued to build houses in the French style even after the French had gone. St Lucians still speak a French-based patois, Kwéyòl, which amalgamated African languages with French and allowed the slaves to communicate with their masters. More than a patois, it has developed into a language in its own right with its own grammatical structure, preserved though wide usage and promoted by radio programmes (see p193). You will hear this spoken around the island by people from all walks of life, particularly in the market where Kwéyòl speakers will receive better prices than others, but English is the language of work, education and the law.

Overall the nation is Caribbean, a melting pot of people and customs and a way of life which encompasses the music of soca, calypso and reggae, carnival and national festivals, Creole cuisine, tropical fruit and rum.

St Lucia is well served with scheduled and charter flights from Europe and North America and you can often pick up quite cheap deals on package holidays. Connections with other islands are good and it is easy to arrange a multi-centre trip. There are two airports. Hewanorra in the south is for long-distance international flights and up to two hours from the beach resorts in the northwest. The smaller, George F Charles airport, often referred to by its former name of Vigie, is used for inter-island short hops and conveniently just outside Castries. You can also get to St Lucia by sea on a scheduled ferry from the French Antilles and Dominica or visit on a cruise ship. The easiest way of seeing the island is by hiring a car, but the mountain roads can be tricky and should be negotiated with caution. Buses run to all the major villages on the island and are cheap, but may not run when you want them to. Taxis are expensive for touring. There are lots of organized tours to out of the way places if you are happy to join a group.

# Getting there

## Air

**From the UK and Europe**  The main carriers from London are **British Airways** (Gatwick), **Virgin Atlantic** (Gatwick) and **BWIA** (Heathrow), with one or other of them flying on Tuesdays, Wednesdays, Fridays and Sundays. **Excel** (www.excelairways.com) and **BMI** (www.flybmi.com) started weekly flights in 2004 from Gatwick and Manchester respectively. Condor comes in once a week with a scheduled service from Frankfurt, but there are many charters running seasonally which offer good package deals with accommodation. Flights from Gatwick start from around £349 in low season but can be double that at holiday times such as Christmas. For cheap deals check the internet (see overleaf for websites).

**From North America and Canada**  Many flights connect in Antigua or Barbados, but there are direct flights with **Air Jamaica, BWIA, US Airways** and **Delta** from New York via Montego Bay from between US$433 and US$558 and **US Airways** from Philadelphia as well as **Air Canada** from Toronto. It can be time consuming flying from somewhere like Boston, Houston or Washington DC with a change of plane in both Miami and Barbados. The cheapest flights from Canada are with **Air Jamaica**, but with two changes you can be travelling for 20 hours. **American Airlines** connects with **American Eagle** in San Juan, which can be quicker.

**Caribbean connections**  There are dozens of daily flights to other islands and to Guyana if you want to island-hop. The main regional airlines are **LIAT**, **Caribbean Star**, **BWIA**, **Air Jamaica** and **American Eagle**. **LIAT** has two passes called *Explorer tickets*. The *LIAT Explorer* costs US$225 (peak season: 1 July-31 August, 5 December-6 January, two weeks around Trinidad Carnival and two weeks around Easter), or US$199 (off-peak: the rest of the year),

### → Airlines

**Air Canada**, **T** 1-888-2472262, www.aircanada.ca
**Air Jamaica**, **T** 1-800-5235585 (North America/Caribbean),
**T** 44-20-85707999 (Europe), www.airjamaica.com
**American Airlines**, **T** 1-800-4337300, www.aa.com
**American Eagle/American Airlines**, **T** 1-800-4337300,
www3.aa.com
**British Airways**, **T** 0845-7733377, www.britishairways.com
**BWIA**, **T** 0870-4992942 (UK/Europe), **T** 1-800-5382942 (North
America), **T** 1-868-6272942 (Caribbean/South America),
www.bwee.com
**Caribbean Star**, **T** 1-800-744STAR, www.flycaribbeanstar.com
**Condor**, **T** 0180-2337135 (Germany), www.condor.de
**Delta**, **T** 800-2414141 (USA), www.delta.com
**LIAT**, **T** 1-268-4805625 (Caribbean), www.liatairline.com
**Virgin Atlantic**, **T** 44-1293-450150, www.virgin-atlantic.com

### Agents

http://travel.kelkoo.co.uk; www.opodo.co.uk
www.cheapflights.com; www.travelocity.com;
www.ebookers.com; wwwstatravel.com

valid for 21 days, maximum four stops permitted at Tortola, San
Juan, Antigua, St Kitts, Nevis, St Thomas, St Croix, St Maarten,
Guadeloupe, Dominica, St Lucia, Barbados, St Vincent, Grenada,
Trinidad and Tobago. The *LIAT Super Caribbean Explorer* costs
US$425 (peak season) or US$399 (off-peak), for a 30-day ticket,
allowing unlimited stop overs in all its Caribbean destinations
except Guyana and the Dominican Republic. **LIAT** also operates an
*Airpass* within the Caribbean except Guyana and Santo Domingo,

in which each flight costs US$75, valid for 21 days, minimum three stopovers. These tickets may only be issued in conjunction with an international flight to a Caribbean gateway; the itinerary must be settled in advance, with no changes permitted, and no child discounts. A return ticket with stopovers is often cheaper than the airpass. **BWIA**'s *Caribbean Airpass* covers all its destinations including Caracas and Paramaribo, but if you include Kingston, Havana, Santo Domingo or San Juan, it will cost more. A first-class unlimited mileage pass is US$750 (US$900 including the four cities listed) and the economy pass is US$450 (US$550). There is also a four-stop pass for US$350 (US$450 three stops to/from Havana, Santo Domingo, San Juan) which can only be bought in the UK, Europe, New Zealand and Australia and you have to travel to the Caribbean with BWIA. You can have any number of stopovers, but no destination may be visited more than once (no 'back-calling'), except for making a connection and the entire journey must be fixed at the time of payment; dates may be left open. This airpass is valid for 30 days; no refunds are given for unused sectors. It may not be used between 19 December and 6 January.

**Airport information** St Lucia has two airports. **George F Charles Airport** (SLU, **T** 4521156), formerly known as Vigie airport, is mainly for inter-island flights (**Caribbean Star**, **Liat**, **BWIA**, **American Eagle** from San Juan, **Air Caraïbes** from the French Antilles with **Air France** connections) and only 2 miles from Castries. A taxi into the capital costs US$7.50.

**Hewanorra International Airport** (UVF, **T** 4546355) is in the Vieux Fort district, where international flights land (**British Airways**, **Virgin Atlantic**, **BWIA**, **Air Canada**, **Air Jamaica** and charter flights). There is an air shuttle to Vigie by **helicopter**, 12 minutes, US$90. Alternatively a **taxi** to Castries costs US$60 (though, out of season, you can negotiate a cheaper rate) and it will take you 1½-2 hours to reach the resorts north of Castries. A cheaper service is the St Lucia Air Shuttle, run by **Paradise Tourist Services**, Rodney

Bay, behind *Julian's Supermarket*, by reservation only, US$17.50 one way, US$33 round trip, per person, credit cards accepted, **T** 4529329, www.stluciatip.com. You can also negotiate a ride with one of the **transfer buses** from hotels for EC$40, enquire at **St Lucia Reps**, **T** 4569100, www.sunlinktours.com. If you are travelling light you can **walk** to the main road and catch the minibus or route taxi to Castries, or walk into Vieux Fort but be careful of the fast traffic. No baggage storage is yet available at Hewanorra. Try to arrange it with one of the Vieux Fort hotels.

Note at both airports there is a **departure tax** of EC$54, US$22, for anyone over 12.

## Sea

*Exprès des Iles* links St Lucia with the French Antilles and Dominica, reservations **T** 4565000, www.express-des-isles.com, or *Cox & Co Ltd*, William Peter Blvd, **T** 4522211. You cannot buy a ticket at the dock, so remember to buy weekend tickets in advance as the office is shut then. Tickets ordered in advance to be collected at the dock, cannot be paid for by credit card. Departs Castries for Fort-de-France Monday 0800, Tuesday 0900 and 1700, Wednesday 1700, Friday 1400, Saturday 0630, Sunday 1300, 1 hour 20 minutes; return Monday 1500, Tuesday 1400, Wednesday 0700, Friday 1200, Saturday 1800, Sunday 1830, EC$183/US$68 day-return plus EC$30, US$12 departure tax. Saturday is the best day for a day trip: you get there in plenty of time for coffee and a croissant, a day's sightseeing and eating well. Customs clearance can be tedious with several hundred passengers. On Wednesday, Saturday and Sunday, the boat continues to Roseau, Dominica (3½ -4 hours) and Pointe-à-Pitre, Guadeloupe (5¾-6¼ hours), returning Friday and Sunday. *Caribbean Ferries*, **T** 4501486, leaves Castries Friday 1415 and Sunday 1430 for Martinique (EC$189 return), Dominica (EC$240) and Guadeloupe (EC$345). The boat returns to Castries Friday 1300 and Sunday 1330, so day trips are not possible but you could spend Friday and Saturday night, or more, on another island for a two-centre holiday. You can also take a yacht or motor launch to Martinique (see p29). Captain Artes of the *S/H Krios*, Rodney Bay Harbour, **T** 4528531, runs a boat taxi (sailing) to Martinique, three days, US$315 plus customs charges; customs officers will make contact for you. Highly recommended. Many cruise lines also call at St Lucia.

**Yachting information** **Ports of entry** and **anchorages** are at Rodney Bay, Castries, Marigot, Soufrière and Vieux Fort. There are **marinas** at Rodney Bay, Castries Yacht Centre and Marigot Bay. **Rodney Bay Marina** is in a lagoon, accessed via a channel between Reduit Beach and Gros Islet, dredged to 15 feet. It is a first-class, full service facility with concrete docks and berths offering water and electricity (220volts/50 cycles) with transformers. Same-day laundry, ice and propane gas are available; within the marina are restaurants, shops, banks, ATMs, public telephones, supermarket and car rental. Customs and Immigration(**T** 4520235) open Saturday to Thursday 0800-1630 and Friday 0800-1800; the Rodney Bay Marina office opens daily 0800-1200, 1300-1800. Castries harbour has two main anchorages: **Vigie Creek** and **Castries City**, the former is the more secluded. **Marigot Bay** has deep water berthing facilities for yachts of up to 200 feet; other yachts can anchor anywhere in the inner harbour. There is water, fuel, ice, laundry facilities, mini-market, shops and restaurants. **The Moorings Yacht Charters** bases 36 charter yachts here. At **Soufrière** anchorages are in the town, at Anse Chastanet and in the north of the bay at the Hummingbird Beach Resort. **The Soufrière Marine Management Area** (**T** 4597200, VHF16, smma@candw.lc) issues *Coral Conservation Permits* to all vessels anchoring within the marine park. **The Soufrière Water Taxi Association** (T4545420) is available for water transfer services and a watchman when boat owners are ashore. At **Vieux Fort**, Customs is at the big ship dock and there are anchorages off there or beside the Fisheries Complex. **Marine Police Unit**, **T** 4522261.

### → Travel extras

**Money** East Caribbean dollar, EC$. EC$2.67=US$1. Banks offer better rates than hotels. The US dollar is accepted in many tourist establishments, but you will receive your change in EC dollars.

**Safety** Harassment and petty crime are the main problems so take the usual precautions: avoid going alone off the beaten track; do not wear expensive jewellery when shopping and stay in well-populated parts of the beach. Never sleep at night on the beach: you will lose your belongings. When visiting the waterfalls and sulphur springs at Soufrière be prepared to say 'no' firmly; 'guides' are sometimes bothersome. Visiting with a hired car (H reg) can be a hassle. Be careful taking photographs, although people seem accustomed to cameras in the market. The use and sale of narcotics is illegal and penalties are severe. Most readily available is marijuana, which is frequently offered to tourists, but hard drugs are also a problem.

**Vaccinations** No vaccination certificates are required except for yellow fever if you are arriving from an infected area.

**Visas** Visitors must carry valid passports except citizens of the USA and Canada, who may enter with adequate proof of identity, as long as they do not stay longer than 6 months. Citizens of the Organization of Eastern Caribbean States (OECS) may enter with only a driving licence or identity card. Visas are not required by nationals of all Commonwealth countries, all EU countries except Eire and Portugal, all Scandinavian countries, Switzerland, Liechtenstein, Turkey, Tunisia, Uruguay and Venezuela. Anyone else needs a visa. Without exception, visitors need a return ticket. You also need an onward address. On arrival you will be given a 42-day stamp in your passport. The immigration office at the central police station in Castries is bureaucratic about extensions; they cost EC$40 per period and it is worth getting one up to the date of your return ticket.

# Getting around

## Bus

Getting around by bus is easy. Hotels and tour operators will encourage you to take a taxi, but this is quite unnecessary during the day, unless you want to get off the beaten track. Bus is the cheapest means of getting around St Lucia. The service has been described as tiresome by some, but as reliable by others. St Lucia's buses are usually privately owned minibuses and have no fixed timetable. The north is better served than the south and buses around Castries and Gros Islet run until 2200, or later for the Friday night jump-up at Gros Islet. Bus stands in Castries are at the bottom of Darling Road on the west side of the gardens and extending back to the multi-storey car park on Peynier Street. Route 1 is Castries to Gros Islet, Route 2 Castries to Vieux Fort, Route 3 Castries to Soufrière, Route 4 Vieux Fort environs, Route 5 Castries central zone. Each route then has sub-routes, eg Route 1A is Castries-Gros Islet, Route 1B is Castries to Babonneau via Union, Route 1D is Castries to Grande Riviere, etc. For Vieux Fort you need 2H or 2I, which will pass Praslin and the Eastern Nature Trail, also Mamiku Gardens. For Anse La Raye via Marigot take 3C or 3D (there is quite a long walk from the main road into Marigot but some buses may make the detour if you ask). For Soufrière only the 3D will do. Short journeys are only EC$1-1.25, rising to EC$2 Castries to Gros Islet, EC$6 Castries to Vieux Fort, EC$9 to Choiseul or to Soufrière, EC$7; from Gros Islet to Rodney Bay EC$1; from Soufrière to Vieux Fort EC$4; with oil prices rising in 2004, fares are expected to go up. Ask the driver to tell you when your stop comes up.

## Car

Drive on the left. Take care at roundabouts if you are not used to it and give way to traffic coming from your right. The use of seat belts is compulsory. The speed limit is 30 mph on highways, 15 mph in towns, although you will be lucky to find anyone keeping to those limits. It is illegal to drive on beaches. Castries roads are very congested and there are more one-way streets than ever. However, you can get on to the new Millennium highway which comes out in Cul de Sac without going into the heart of Castries. There are several car hire companies on the island, see p173, some of which are open to negotiation, but it is cheaper and more reliable to hire in advance. Car hire is about US$45-95 per day, depending on the size of the vehicle, with discounts for weekly rates. The minimum age for car rental is 25. Optional collision damage waiver is another US$10-22 per day. A 5% tax is added to everything. A one-day licence costs US$12, or US$20 for up to three months. If arriving at George F L Charles (formerly Vigie) Airport, get your international licence endorsed at the immigration desk (closed 1300-1500) after going through customs. Car hire companies can usually arrange a licence. Most have offices at the hotels, airports and in Castries. Check for charges for pick-up and delivery. If dropping off a car at George F L Charles Airport you can sometimes leave the keys with the tourist desk if there is no office for your car hire company. Filling stations are open Monday-Saturday 0630-2000, selected garages open Sunday and holidays 1400-1800. They only sell unleaded fuel, at EC$8.75 per US gallon.

## Cycling
If you're cycling, the best way to get round the island is anti-clockwise, thus ensuring long but gradual uphills and steep, fast downhills. Watch out for pot holes and cars coming round a bend on the wrong side of the road. Cycling has become popular, mostly in groups with a guide, see Cycling tours, p30, Bicycle hire p173.

## Ferries
*Rodney Bay Ferry* shuttles between the marina shops, Marlin Quay, St Lucian Hotel, Mortar and Pestle and Pigeon Island, fares within the marina US$8 return, children under 12 half price, **T** 4520087, also half-day trips to Pigeon Island including lunch, US$40,

bookings at the yellow hut by the entrance to Lime Restaurant's car park. Jerome, **T** 3841961, will take you from Eagle's Inn to Pigeon Island for EC$10. The *Gingerbread Express* in Marigot Bay costs EC$5 return, but is refunded by Doolittle's Restaurant if you eat or drink there and present your tickets. Water taxis and speedboats can be rented. Water taxis ply between Soufrière waterfront and Anse Chastanet, easier than driving the awful road.

## Taxi

Registered taxis have red number plates with the TX prefix. Minibuses have the T prefix. Fares are set by the government, but the US$60 Castries-Soufrière fare doubles as unlucky tourists discover that there are no buses for the return journey. Club St Lucia, in the extreme north, to Castries, about 10 miles away, costs US$15-18 one way for one-four people, US$3.75 per additional passenger. Fare from Castries to Gros Islet (for Friday evening street party), US$12; to Pigeon Island National Park, US$15.50 one way; to Vigie Airport, US$5; to Hewanorra Airport, US$56; Vigie Airport to Rodney Bay US$16; Marigot Bay to Hewanorra Airport US$45; to Vigie Airport US$22, to Castries US$20 (30 minutes). If in doubt about the amount charged, check with the tourist office or hotel reception. You can see a copy of the fixed fares at the airport. At rush hour it is almost impossible to get a taxi so allow plenty of time; the traffic jams are amazing for such a small place.

## Walking

Hiking is rewarding on St Lucia as the views are stunning and there are lots of birds and plants to see. There are many hiking trails of varying degrees of difficulty through the mountains and rainforest, see Walking tours, p31. On the road, remember to walk on the right so that you can see approaching vehicles. Accidents have happened and the Gablewoods Mall area is dangerous if crossing the road. Avoid walking on the road at night as there is often nowhere to get off and oncoming cars travel very fast.

# Tours

## Air tours

**St Lucia Helicopters** at Pointe Seraphine, **T** 4536950, offer tours of the north or south of the island. From Pointe Seraphine a north island helicopter tour costs US$45, 10 minutes; south island US$80, 20 minutes; a heli-hike with tour of Atlantic beaches and Cactus Valley US$65, **T** 4500806; helicopters can also be hired for airport transfers, US$100 from Pointe Seraphine to Hewanorra, also pick-up from some hotels.

## Boat tours

Some of the best views are from the sea. Anse Chastanet, Jalousie, Windjammer Landing and Sandals have their own boats: spend an evening cruising into the sunset with as much champagne as you can drink. Several boats sail down the west coast from Rodney Bay to Soufrière, where you stop to visit the volcano and a waterfall, followed by lunch and return sail with a pause for swimming and snorkelling. The price usually includes all transport, lunch, drinks and snorkelling gear. The *Unicorn* is a 140-ft replica of a 19th-century brig which started life in 1947 as a Baltic trader (used in the filming of *Roots* and *Pirates of the Caribbean*), **T** 4526811. Sailings are 0930 Monday-Friday in high season, US$90 per person, children under 12 US$45, including lunch. Champagne and sunset cruises available on Monday, Wednesday, Friday 1700-1900, adults, US$45, children US$23. You can also book through hotel tour desks. Other excursions on catamarans (*Endless Summer I*, *Endless Summer II*, *Tout Bagay*) and private yachts can be booked with tour operators in Castries or through the hotels. The catamarans can be overcrowded and devoid of character but cost the same as the *Unicorn*. An alternative is to charter a yacht with skipper and mate. Motor boats can also be chartered for customized trips including fishing and snorkelling. A day charter costs US$400 for one to four people, with a capacity for up to eight more at US$5 per person.

● *At the swimming stop local divers may try to sell you coral. This is illegal.*

There are also day sails to neighbouring islands: Martinique US$95, Dominica US$215, Grenadines including sail, US$199-295, Barbados US$230. Don't forget to take your passport. A day trip to Martinique on the catamaran, *Flying Ray*, leaves Rodney Bay Marina at 0730, returning at around 1730. You can tour Fort-de-France with a guide or on your own, then the boat continues to Anse Noire for a barbeque lunch and rum punch. You can swim and snorkel here then cruise back past Diamond Rock and watch out for dolphins in the channel between Martinique and St Lucia. On Saturdays day trips run to Martinique with *Exprès des Iles*, see p22.

Whale-watching tours can be done with **Hackshaw's Boat Charters** (Chris), **T** 4530553. The cost is US$50 plus transfers. **Captain Mike's** (Mike Hackshaw) also does whale watching as well as sport fishing and pleasure cruises. They use a 55-ft boat, *Free Willy*, which has an upper and lower deck for viewing, and the trip lasts three hours, **T** 4527044, www.captmikes.com.

### Bus tours

Most hotels will arrange tours (US$40-80) to the island's principal attractions around Soufrière either by road, boat or helicopter. Coach tours are cheaper and usually daily in high season, falling to once or twice a week off season. A full-day tour booked through a tour agency will be around US$60. The main tour agencies are **St Lucia Reps/Sunlink Tours**, **T** 4528232, www.stluciareps.com; **Spice Travel**, **T** 4520866, www.casalucia.com; **Solar Tours**, **T** 4519041; **Barnards Travel**, **T** 4522214; **Barefoot Holidays**, **T** 4500507, www.travelfile.com/get/baredays.html. Local tour operators also offer plantation tours; Errard and Balenbouche offer fascinating insights into colonial history and local environments. A tour of a working banana plantation is recommended, you see a lot of the country and see and taste a lot of native fruit and vegetables.

## Cycling tours

**Carib Travel**, **T** 4522151, have 15 Rockhoppers and offer a trip from Paix Bouche through mountain villages down to Gros Islet. **Island Bike Hikes**, **T** 4580908, www.cyclestlucia.com, run vehicle-supported and tailor-made bike tours from US$58, a great way to explore the beaches of the northeast coast. **Bike St Lucia**, **T** 4597755, www.bikestlucia.com, on a beach just north of Anse Chastanet (linked to *Scuba St Lucia*), offer off-road riding on trails through 400 acres of forest (jungle biking). They have a fleet of Cannondale F800 CAAD-3 bikes, which are not for use away from their trails. Accessible only by boat, they organize transfers from your hotel, lunch, snorkelling, US$89. **Jungle Reef Adventures**, **T** 4571400, is a combination of *Scuba St Lucia* and *Bike St Lucia*, offering sea kayaking, snorkelling, diving and cycling; tour prices US$59-99 include transport, showers, lockers and buffet lunch.

## Heritage tours

**St Lucia Heritage Tours**, **T** 4516058 at Pointe Seraphine, **T** 4515067 at La Place Carenage, heritagetours@candw.lc. Heritage Tours were developed to give greater community involvement in environmentally sustainable tourism. All the sites are privately owned but developed to an acceptable standard and supported by the government. If you book a tour you can visit a number of places including Latille Falls (20-foot waterfall and pools where you can swim), Fond d'Or Nature and Historical Park (hiking trails to plantation house ruins, Amerindian remains and the beach), Fond Latisab Créole Park (traditional methods of making cassava bread), Fond Doux (19th-century plantation house and nature trails through fruit gardens, where the Battle of Rabot was fought) and the Folk Research Centre (19th-century building on Mount Pleasant documenting Kwéyòl culture and history). A Castries Heritage Walk covers the architectural history of the city. Costs vary from US$12 for Castries to US$69 for a day tour to Soufrière, Toraille Falls, the volcano and lunch at Fond Doux Estate.

## Rum tours
**St Lucia Distillers**, south towards Marigot, **T** 4514258, has an excellent rum factory tour, *Rhythm of Rum*, with tasting, shop for purchases. Monday-Friday 0900-1500, US$10 plus transfers. A variety of rum products are made here, from white to aged rum and blended drinks. In a joint venture with the French West Indies, they also bottle La Belle Creole liqueurs.

## Taxi tours
A trip round the island by taxi is about US$20 per hour for one-four people, with an additional US$5 per hour for air conditioning. Recommended taxi drivers are Kenneth James, **T** 4536844, **T** 4519778, Barnard Henry, **T** 4501951, Samson Louis, **T** 4500516 (or through the Rex St Lucian taxi stand) and Raymond Cepal, pager **T** 4843583. In Vieux Fort, Winson Edward at the **New Frontier Taxi Association**, **T** 4549156, will organize guided tours.

## Walking tours
The **Forestry Department** organizes hiking across the island. Contact Adams Toussaint, **T** 4502231 ext 306 or **T** 4502078, who is in charge of all Forestry Department tours. Donald Anthony, a senior Forestry Officer, is also available as a private guide for hikers and bird watchers, contact him at Forestry or **T** 4521799. You need a permit from the Forestry Department for walking in the national parks, US$10 (US$5 for children). Tours are franchised to tour operators and a guide is certainly useful but organized tours are often noisy. Get your own permit from the Forestry Department if you feel confident about finding your own way.

The **St Lucia National Trust** (**T** 4525005) has fairly regular field trips, usually the last Sunday of the month, popular with locals and tourists of all ages. The cost varies according to transport costs, membership US$10 a year.

**Wilderness Explorers**, www.wilderness-explorers.com, also specialize in nature as well as adventure travel.

# Tourist information

**St Lucia Tourist Board**, Sure Line Building, on main Castries-Gros Islet highway just north of the Vigie roundabout, Castries, St Lucia, **T** 4524094, F4531121, www.stlucia.org. Information centres at the Pointe Seraphine Duty-Free Complex; La Place Carenage; George F Charles Airport (most helpful but closed for lunch 1300-1500), **T** 4522596; Hewanorra Airport (very helpful, particularly with hotel reservations, only open when flights are due or leave), **T** 4546644 and on the waterfront in Soufrière, **T** 4597419.

**Tourist offices abroad** include: 1 Collingham Gardens, London SW5 0HW, **T** 0870-9007697, sltbinfo@stluciauk.org; 800 Second Av, 9th floor, New York, NY 10017, **T** 212-8672950, 1-800-4563984, stluciatourism@aol.com; 8 King St East, Suite 700, Toronto, Ontario M5C 1B5, **T** 416-3624242, 1-800-8690377, sltbcanada@aol.com.

The *Tropical Traveller* is distributed free to hotels, shops and restaurants every month and contains some extremely useful information, www.tropicaltraveller.com. The St Lucia Hotel and Tourism Associations publishes a tourist guide, *Visions of St Lucia*, **T** 4525978, www.stluciatravel.com.lc, also of a high standard and widely available. For yachties the monthly *Compass* is available free from some outlets. The Rodney Bay Village Association distributes *Village Voice*, a newsletter with what's on where.

## Maps

Maps of the island may be obtained from the Land Survey in the last government building. At 1:50,000 they are the best but not 100% accurate. *Ordnance Survey*, Romsey Rd, Southampton, UK (**T** 01703-792792), produce a map of St Lucia in their World Maps series which includes tourist information such as hotels, beaches, climbing and climate. Small commercial maps are available free in hotels. *Skyviews Road Map & Guide*, www.skyviews.com, is updated regularly and has town maps of Rodney Bay, Castries and Soufrière as well as an island map and tourist information with advertising.

# The Island

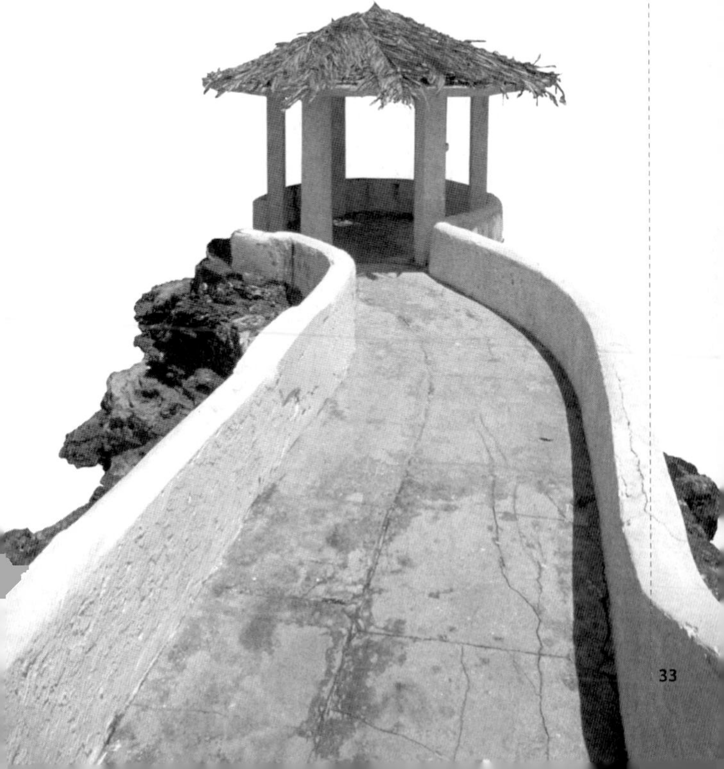

## Castries, 35

The capital city – a busy port on one of the Caribbean's most beautiful natural harbours.

## North to Rodney Bay and Gros Islet, 45

The most developed area with good beaches, hotels, restaurants, nightlife, sporting facilities and the marina.

## The north and northeast coasts, 50

A quiet area in the driest part of the island with some luxury villas and wild beaches – the place to come for turtle watching.

## East coast to Vieux Fort, 55

The dramatic Atlantic coast with its cliffs, bays, tiny islands offshore, fishing villages and access to the rainforest walks for birdwatching and hiking and the best beach for kiteboarding

## West coast to Soufrière and the Pitons, 69

Stunning mountain scenery and dozens of pretty bays make this the most beautiful part of the island and unmissable. Sulphur springs and excellent snorkelling and diving in the marine reserve.

# Castries

The capital, Castries, is splendidly set on a natural harbour against a background of mountains. It used to be guarded by the great fortress of **Morne Fortune** (Fort Charlotte and Derrière Fort) up on the steep hills to the south of the town. There is a spectacular view from the road just below Morne Fortune where the town appears as a kaleidoscope of colour: red roofs contrasting with the blue of the sea and the green of the mountains.

Named by the British after the Maréchal de Castries, a French governor in 1780, the port was developed in the second half of the 19th century for coal bunkering. Welsh coal was brought to St Lucia and sold on to passing steam ships, so that by the turn of the century Castries was the 14th most important port in the world in terms of tonnage handled. By the 1930s oil had superseded coal and the port declined. In 1948 most of the town was engulfed in flames and many buildings destroyed when a fire started in a tailor's shop, although fortunately there was no loss of life. Further fires caused damage in 1951 and 1963 and, as a result, the commercial centre and government offices have been largely reconstructed and are built of concrete. Only the buildings to the south of **Derek Walcott Square** and behind **Brazil Street** were saved. Here you will see late 19th- and early 20th-century wooden buildings built in French style with three storeys, their gingerbread fretwork balconies overhanging the pavement. The tallest building in the city is the seven-storey Financial Centre at the corner of Jeremie and Bridge Streets, with a joyous sculpture by local artist, Ricky George.

Nowadays, buoyed by tourism, the port is thriving again, receiving some of the largest craft in the world: cruise ships. The city centre is very crowded when cruise ships come in and the **market** becomes a hive of activity. There are duty-free shopping centres for cruise ship passengers at La Place Carenage by the main dock and at **Pointe Seraphine** to the north.

*Castries is small and all the sights of interest in the centre can easily be visited on foot in a morning. Getting up to Morne Fortune, though, is easier in a car. It is no problem to get out of Castries using public transport as the minibuses start from near the market to villages all over the island. Just to the east of Vigie, parallel with the beach, is the the George FL Charles airport for regional flights, usually known as Vigie airport.*

➡ *See Sleeping p91, Eating and drinking p113*

##  Sights

### The market

On the north side of Jeremie Street   *Open daily, Saturday is the busiest day, particularly during Carnival or the Jazz Festival Map 2, F3 and F4, p206   See also p147*

The market is a lively central place to start a tour of the city, to pick up the odd souvenir and to sample local food as eaten by St Lucians – the food stalls are a good bet for an authentic, wholesome lunch. If you are self-catering then you might be tempted to buy some of the wonderful tropical fruit and vegetables on offer, with various ground provisions (root vegetables), christophene, breadfruit or green banana (fig) being sold by farmers. Watch to see what prices St Lucians are being charged so that you can get the same. In the craft market you can bargain for a good price.

The original market was constructed entirely of iron in 1894, conceived by Mr Augier, member of the Town Board, and built by engineers Bruce and Steel Ltd, of Liverpool, to enhance the appearance of the town and also provide a sheltered place where fruit and produce could be sold hygienically. However, a century later the market had outgrown its building so a new market has been built next door on two floors, in which are housed the many fruit sellers and vendors of T-shirts, crafts, spices, basket work, leeches and hot pepper sauce. The array of spices is quite staggering and the basket displays are very tempting, with enormous chunks of cinnamon bark, aromatic cocoa sticks, handfuls of shiny brown nutmegs and pretty bottles of ground spices and sauces.

● *Buying a coal pot is also a favourite souvenir, if you can work out how to carry it home. This is a clay bowl which sits on top of a clay oven, rather like a mini barbeque, and comes in several sizes.*

On the eastern side of the old market there is a little arcade with small booths where vendors provide good vegetarian food, Creole meals and local juices.

Further west along Jeremie Street on what used to be called the Northern Wharf on the waterfront is a large new shopping centre with duty-free shops: **La Place Carenage**. Cruise ship passengers pass through here when disembarking. There are jewellers, internet access, gift shops and craft shops, see Shopping, p143.

## Derek Walcott Square
*Map 2, G3, p206*

A green and pleasant 2 ½-acre square dominated by a giant Saman tree in the middle, known locally as *massave*, believed to be about 400 years old, and the **Roman Catholic Cathedral** to the east. To the west at the corner of Bourbon and Micoud Streets sits the neo-classical **Central Library**, one of several built by US millionaire Andrew Carnegie. Elegant, balconied houses, once the homes of the upper classes in colonial times, surround the square, at one of which, **Kimlan's** restaurant, you can sit on the balcony with a drink or lunch and watch the world go by. Always the principal square of the town,

!   Legend has it that the Saman tree got its local name, *massave*, when a boy was asked the name of the tree by a visitor. Not knowing, he said in Kwéyòl, *"mwen pas save"* ( "I don't know"), but the visitor thought he said *massave*.

Derek Walcott Square was the Place d'Armes in 1768 when the town transferred from Petit Carénage and Vigie and was the original site of the courthouse (demolished in the 19th century) and the market. It has evolved through many name changes: Promenade Square, then controversially Columbus Square in 1893 and more recently in 1993 it was renamed in honour of poet Derek Walcott, see p190, and contains busts of both of St Lucia's Nobel Laureates as well as a white war memorial. The square is used for ceremonial occasions and entertainment.

● *Nowadays it hosts several concerts during the Jazz Festival, called* Jazz on the Square, *as well as other musical events.*

### Cathedral of the Immaculate Conception
Micoud St and Laborie St. *Mass Sat 1930, Sun 0600, 0730, children's Mass 1000, evening service 1800. Map 2, G3, p206*

On the east side of Derek Walcott Square lies the Roman Catholic Cathedral, which bursts into colour inside. Suffused with yellow light from stained-glass windows high up, the side altars are often covered with flowers while votive candles placed in red, green and yellow jars give a fairy-tale effect. The ceiling, supported by delicate iron arches and braces, is decorated with large panelled portraits of the apostles. Above the central altar with its four carved screens, the apse ceiling has paintings of five female saints with St Lucy in the centre. The walls have murals by Dunstan St Omer, one of St Lucia's better known artists (see p187) and are unusual in that the people in the paintings are black. On the pillars are more paintings, of the stations of the cross – there is very little in the church which is not painted except the gallery where the choir sits. The presbytery next door survived the fire of 1948 despite being built of timber because the cathedral served as a fire break. It has a good example of the double-angled mansard roof.

## Brazil Street
*Map 2, G2-5, p206*

The buildings on Brazil Street survived the fire of 1948 and are thus still a fine example of French colonial architecture bordering the Derek Walcott Square. Some of them have been renovated and turned into shops, but the façades are in keeping with the other old buildings. Two of the most interesting are **Kaycees** and the former **Rain** restaurant, with their latticed overhanging balconies and gingerbread fretwork. East of the square there are some fine examples of **chattel houses**. These buildings, made of wood on a stone base, were a forerunner of mobile homes. They were designed and built in such a way that they could be easily dismantled and moved wherever work took their inhabitants – families moved with 'all their goods and chattels'. They traditionally have two rooms, with the front door slightly off centre, shuttered windows and are brightly painted. Further along on the corner with Brogile Street is the **Pink House** (see Architecture, p186), formerly the home of a prominent politician with a pharmacy on the ground floor, but now used as shops with a restaurant upstairs. The building has a magnificent covered balcony on stilts all around the first floor, providing shade for street goers below, with typical French colonial latticework decorating the balcony. The **Castries Heritage Walk** organized by the National Trust with Heritage Tours always includes Brazil Street, see p30

## Folk Research Centre
La Pansée Rd, Mount Pleasant, Castries, **T** 4522279. *Mon-Fri, 0830-1630. Up in the hills just east of Castries. Follow signs to Cara Suites Hotel; it is on the right as you go up the hill.* *Map 2, F6, p206*

The Folk Research Centre is in an old manor house originally owned by the Devaux family (see p77) and is a fine example of colonial architecture, with its verandas and gingerbread fretwork.

The centre is dedicated to documenting the language and culture of St Lucia and has done much to preserve Kwéyòl and make it a written as well as a spoken language. There is a small museum with a collection of musical instruments, and a research library with books and photographs on folklore and history.

## Pointe Seraphine

On the outskirts on the northern side of the harbour near the port. *Mon-Fri 0800-1630. Take the John Compton Highway north towards Vigie Airport and branch off just past the fish market. Plenty of people who will 'mind your car' here. Ignore them. Ferry from La Place Carenage every 10 mins, US$1. Map 2, D1, p206 See also p148*

Pointe Seraphine is a **duty-free complex** near the port. All the usual gift shops and jewellers are here and passengers off the cruise ships which stop this side of the harbour often go no further. The approach is protected by a barrier to stop entry by unauthorised vehicles. The unusual pyramid-shaped building is the **Alliance Française cultural centre**, built in 1993 to further relations between the French and St Lucian people.

## Vigie

*Map 1, C3, p204*

Castries harbour is protected on three sides by hills, of which the Vigie promontory is one. The word Vigie comes from the French term for having someone posted as lookout and both the French and the English saw its strategic purpose and built defensive military positions there. The **Vigie Lighthouse** was built in 1914 by Chance Brothers and Co Ltd, although a lookout of sorts was used as far back as 1768. Its light can be seen 30 miles out to sea. **Vigie beach** (1½ miles from Castries) is a lovely strip of sand with plenty of shade, popular and cleaned regularly. Its only drawback is that it runs parallel to the airport runway but that is compensated by the lack of hotels (except *Rendezvous* at one end). The airport is used for inter-island flights with small aircraft, so they don't take long to take off or land and the noise soon passes.

## Morne Fortune

*The National Trust offers tours of the Morne Fortune Historic Area. Buses go up the Morne on their way south. From the town centre, head south down Micoud Street then turn right into Government House Road, up the hill and onto Morne Road. Very twisty and steep, dangerous to walk because of traffic negotiating the bends.*
*Map 1, D4, p204*

The ridge of Morne Fortune just south of the city centre enjoys wonderful views over Castries and the harbour and receives pleasant breezes to temper the tropical sunshine. For this reason the British built their grand houses up here as well as their military buildings. **Government House** with its curious metalwork crown, is at the top of Morne Fortune, about a mile from Castries at a height of 133 m (437 ft). There has been a Government House up here since the military buildings were transferred up from Vigie, but not always on the same spot. Hurricanes and disease snuffed out governors and houses alike: four governors alone died in the wooden house known as the Pavilion between1829-34. The current incarnation of Government House was completed in1895 and considered a gross waste of public money at the huge cost of £8,800. Unfortunately it is no longer open to the public except by prior arrangement. However, there is a small museum installed by the Governor General, Dame Pearlette Louisy, called **Le Pavillon Royal Museum, T** 4522481, www.stluciagovernmenthouse.com, *(open Tue and Thu 1000-1200, 1400-1600, but check hours, no charge but there is a box for donations)*, with a collection of photos, artefacts and documents.

There are six historical **military sites** on Morne Fortune under the control of the National Trust of St Lucia, www.slunatrust.org

They were built for obvious strategic reasons as you can see most of the northwest coast and the town from the top of the 260-m hill. The fortifications were started by the French in 1768, but expanded and completed by the British. Most of the buildings and the ruins are being used for housing or educational purposes. **Fort Charlotte**, the old Morne Fortune fortress, is now the Sir Arthur Lewis Community College.

The **Apostles' Battery** (1888-90) was built by the British long after the threat from France had gone, but at a time when the port was important as a coaling station and the harbour needed protecting. It was built at ground level so you couldn't see it from the sea. There are four cannons, each weighing four tons, and the National Trust is trying to restore the site. The **Powder Magazine** was constructed in the mid-18th century by the French to store gunpowder and is probably the oldest building in St Lucia which is still intact. **Prevost's Redoubt** (1782) was a lookout point and from here you can see as far as Martinique on a clear day. It was named after Brigadier General Prevost, who was Governor of St Lucia 1798-1802 when the effect of the French Revolution was being felt in the islands and there was great insecurity. Next to the lookout an open patch of grassland is planned as a National Heroes Park and Monument. The French (the oldest, dating from 1782) and British **cemeteries** are beside each other in a residential area. Some five British and one French governor are buried here, as well as military personnel and civilians, many of whom died of malaria and yellow fever. The **Guard Cells** are all that is left of the Officers' Quarters and stables built by the French at the end of the 18th century and may have been used as prison cells for soldiers who had committed crimes.

The most spectacular **view** is from the **Inniskilling Monument** at the far side of the college (just beyond the old Combermere barracks) over the town, coast, mountains and Martinique. It was here in 1796 that General Moore launched an attack on the French who, together with the Brigands had gained control of the island after defeating the British at Vieux Fort and Rabot. The steep slopes give some idea of how fierce the two days of fighting must have been. As a rare honour, the 27th Inniskilling Fusiliers were allowed to fly their regimental flag for one hour after they took the fortress before the Union Jack was raised. The monument was built at the eastern end of Fort Charlotte in 1932 to commemorate the event. Sir Arthur Lewis, Nobel Laureate in Economics, is buried in front of the Inniskilling Monument.

● *There are two very good places for lunch or dinner on The Morne, see p114. Eudovics Art Studio is also worth a visit, see p145.*

### La Toc

Bagshaw's Studio **T** 4527921  *Mon-Fri 0830-1600, Sat 0830-1200.* La Toc Battery  **T** 4526039,  *daily 0900-1500; for information or a tour call Alice Bagshaw, or enquire at the shop. On returning to Castries, branch left at Government House to visit La Toc Point.*
*Map 1, C3, p204  See also p145*

Take the road to the luxury *Sandals* hotel through its beautiful gardens and the path to the right of the security gate if you want to visit the beach. Further on is the road leading to **Bagshaw's studio**, where you can buy attractive silkscreen clothes and household linens and visit the printshop to watch the screen printing process. The company is very highly regarded and has even been commissioned to make prints for Queen Elizabeth II and outfits for her grandsons, Princes William and Harry. Carry your return air ticket for a discount. Close to Bagshaw's is **La Toc Battery**, the best restored military fort of the 60 forts around Castries, visited mostly by cruise-ship visitors. It is owned, maintained and run by Alice Bagshaw and kept in pristine condition. There are cannon on the thick walls, underground rooms and corridors with exhibits of artefacts found in and around the area, including a collection of over 900 bottles found by diving in Castries harbour. It was completed in 1888 to repel a potential attack from the USA when Castries was still a valuable coaling harbour. However, as the threat disappeared, the fort was abandoned from 1905 until Alice Bagshaw bought it in 1982.

### Forestière Rainforest Trail

Forestry Department, Forestière, **T** 4516168, forestrails@slumaffe.org   *Guides available Mon-Fri, 0830-1500. Pay on site, US$10. Guides can be arranged at weekends but will cost more. 20 mins' drive from Castries. Bus 5D from Castries.*
*Map 1, D5, p204   See also Kids p163*

This 3-mile, two-hour trail is part of an old French road that used to run from Castries down to Gros Islet and you can still see the stone walls, terracing and paving. However, parts are quite narrow and you wonder how they got a horse and cart along it. The trail is popular with tour operators, who bring parties here in the mornings, so come in the afternoon for a quieter time. It is a good introduction to the rainforest with lots of huge fig trees, epiphytes and ferns. The guide will point out incense trees oozing white sap with a pungent smell. Good for photo opportunities is the chataignier tree with its enormous buttresses. There is an old bat roost on the trail, but unfortunately the bats have left home after having been disturbed by too much flash photography. Another trail goes up from here to Piton Flore, see p58, taking about two hours.

# North to Rodney Bay and Gros Islet

*The part of the island to the north of Castries is the principal resort area, with the best **beaches**, lots of **hotels** and most of the **nightlife** and entertainment. **Rodney Bay** is the centre of activities and also contains a large marina attracting cruising yachts and the yachtie crowd. There are lots of watersports on offer and it is a good place for a family holiday. On the other side of the marina, **Gros Islet** is more of a village, with guest houses, bars and rum shops, coming alive on Friday nights for its weekly jump-up. **Pigeon Island** is of historical interest, having been a British military base in colonial times, but it is also a beautiful spot on a promontory with good views of the northwest coast.*

*The John Compton highway leaves Castries past Vigie Airport and follows the curves of Vigie Beach and **Choc Bay** up to Rodney Bay and Gros Islet.*

▸▸ *See Sleeping p94, Eating and drinking p115, Bars and clubs p128*

 Sights

---

### Beaches from Castries to Rodney Bay

*All the beaches can be reached by bus with a short walk down to the sea. Bus 1A for all places up to Rodney Bay, 1A, 1B (Babonneau via Union) and 1D (Grande Rivière) as far as Choc and 1A, 1D or 1E (which goes to Monchy) for the Marisule Beach and 1A and 1E for the East Winds and Windjammer turnoffs. There is a bus stop just past the turning to Gros Islet and transport beyond this point to Cap and the causeway and Pigeon Island is possible.*

All the west coast beaches have good swimming but many are dominated by resort hotels.

**Choc Bay** has good sand, shade and chairs provided by the restaurant, *Wharf* (get off the bus after *Sandals Halcyon*) close to *Gablewoods Mall*. Used mainly by cruise ship passengers and locals, there are kayaks, sea cycles and sunfish for hire *(daily, 0900-1800)*. **Marisule** is a small, rocky beach, good for local colour with fishing boats and nets. **Labrellotte Bay** is the location for the up-market *East Winds* and *Windjammer Landing* hotels. **Trouya** is a small, usually deserted bay (except on public holidays), best reached on foot or by 4WD. The northern part of Rodney Bay is cut off by the marina and is now a 45-minute walk or a short bus ride to Gros Islet. There are more beaches on the way to **Pigeon Point**, with ample shade and two small beaches on Pigeon Island itself.

● *Choc is a style of Amerindian pottery decoration including finger-indented rims, clay masks and figurines, clay stamps for designs using plant dyes and large footed griddles for baking cassava bread.*

---

### Union Agricultural Station

Forestry Department, **T** 4502231 Ext 316, www.geocities.com/sluforestrails or contact Adams Toussaint on Ext 306 or any of his knowledgeable team, see p31. *Where the John Compton Highway leaves Choc Bay and just before it crosses the Choc River, a right turn to Babonneau will take you past the Union Agricultural station (about 1 mile). Bus 1B from Castries. Map 1, C5, p204 See also Kids p166*

---

Union is the site of the Forestry Department headquarters, where there is a visitor centre, nature trail and a small, well-run zoo. The hillside trail is a 1-mile loop through tropical dry forest, reaching an elevation of 107 m (350 ft). There are some steps and rough ground but it is an easy walk at a leisurely pace of about a couple of hours. The garden trail is a ½-mile stroll through the overgrown medicinal herb garden. The mini zoo offers an opportunity to see indigenous species such as the agouti and the endemic St Lucia parrot as well as species which have been introduced.

**!** The Caribs called St Lucia *louanalao*, the island of the iguanas.

▶ **Eats shoots and leaves**

## St Lucia iguana

The iguana is the largest of the lizards found on St Lucia, growing up to 2 m ( about 6 ft) long including the tail. It is mostly green, with brown or black stripes, nose horns and a crest of long spines along the neck. Females lay up to 17 eggs in the ground which take around 14 weeks to hatch.

Iguanas are vegetarians, eating leaves, shoots and fruit. They live in trees but can also be seen on the ground. Numbers are decreasing because of predation by mongooses and feral cats.

They are found on the northeast coast around Louvet and Grand Anse.

## Agouti

A member of the rodent family, the agouti is a mammal indigenous to St Lucia. It has coarse brown hair and sits erect on long thin legs. The agouti is nocturnal, living in open country on the edge of forests and feeding on leaves, roots, fruit and nuts. It reproduces twice a year, having two or three babies in each litter, which are born fully active.

Like all St Lucia's wildlife (except the fer-de-lance, mongoose, rats and mice), agoutis were declared a protected species in 1980 after they became scarce, but there are several in the zoo, born in captivity.

The Forestry Department organizes hiking across the island through rainforest and mature mahogany, Caribbean pine and blue mahoe plantations which will give you the best chance of seeing the St Lucia parrot, as well as other rainforest birds: thrashers, vireos, hummingbirds, flycatchers, etc.

## Rodney Bay

*Pass through the entrance gates of the old Naval Air Station or take the next left turn off the main road at the junction leading to JQ's Mall, to reach the hotels and restaurants. Bus 1A from Castries. The Rodney Bay Ferry, **T** 4528816, runs between the marina and the shops hourly 0900-1600 for US$4. Map 1, A5, p204 and Map 3, p207*

Today this whole area supports a mass of tourist facilities - hotels, restaurants, shops and clubs - between the lovely beach at Reduit and the first-class Rodney Bay Marina, but it was formerly the site of the US Naval Air Station of Reduit. Built in 1941, the Americans made an attempt to reclaim the mangrove swamps and the bay was dredged. It was the first of a chain of bases established to protect the Panama Canal and supported a squadron of sea planes. Closed in 1947 it was not until much later when a causeway and marina were built that the wetlands vanished.

If you drive to the end of the road past all the restaurants and night spots there is good access to the beach at **Reduit**. This is an excellent base for **watersports**; it is ideal for windsurfing, although dominated by the *Papillon*, *Rex St Lucian* (parasailing) and *Royal St Lucian* hotels. You can use their bars and sports-hire facilities but it is crowded with guests. The Rodney Bay Development Company is developing the area further.

## Gros Islet

*45-min walk or 5- to 10-min bus ride from Rodney Bay. Bus 1A from Castries  Map 1, A5, p204*

The other side of the marina outlet, Gros Islet has none of the tourist trappings of Rodney Bay. It is full of little wooden shacks, painted in pastel colours and has the atmosphere of a village, not a resort. There are guest houses and lots of little bars along the beach and in the village, but these are cheap and cheerful and you get what you pay for. The 19th-century church of St Joseph the

Worker is grey and unattractive, although the cemetery has views of Pigeon Island, but alongside is a pretty, newly restored, pink bell tower, which is worth a look. The normally sleepy fishing village holds a popular **jump-up** in the street each Friday night, from 2200, with music, dancing, bars, cheap food and more tourists than locals but good fun all the same. Dozens of barbecues sell fried chicken and bake, kebabs or corn on the cob. Try the grilled conch from one of the booths selling local dishes. You shouldn't experience any problems, but leave your valuables at home and don't encourage pickpockets; don't stray down unlit alleyways and stay away from anyone offering drugs.

## Pigeon Island

*Daily 0900-1700; museum closed Sun. Entry to park and museum EC$10 visitors, EC$5 residents (free after 1700 but only to the restaurants). About ¾ mile after Elliot's Shell station on the outskirts of Gros Islet, turn left.The Rodney Bay Ferry, **T** 4528816, goes to Pigeon Island twice daily from The Lime restaurant. Round-trip transport, entry fee, lunch costs US$50.* Map 1, A4, p204 See also Kids p166

Pigeon Island National Historic Park is a lovely spot on the promontory. Once an island, it is now joined to the mainland by a causeway on which a hideous 300-room hotel (*Sandals Grande*) has been built with a bright blue roof and custard coloured walls. There are a couple of beaches open to the public on the causeway, either side of Sandals. The first of these will no doubt be developed with more hotels in the future but for now it is used by locals who come and relax here, buy cheap chicken and beer and play dominoes on the beach.

● *It is a good place to be on New Year's Eve when you can watch all the fireworks around the bay.*

The beach between Sandals and Pigeon Point is public domain and can't be built on. The park on Pigeon Island was opened by Princess Alexandra on 23 February 1979 as part of St Lucia's

Independence celebrations. It has two peaks joined by a saddle. The higher rises to a height of about 109 m (359 ft). Managed by the National Trust, the island is of considerable archaeological and historical interest. Amerindian remains have been found, the French pirate François Leclerc (known as 'Jambe de Bois' for his wooden leg) used the large cave on the north shore and the Duke of Montagu tried to colonize it in 1722 (but abandoned it after one afternoon). From here, Admiral Rodney set sail in 1782 to meet the French navy at the Battle of Les Saintes. The island was also captured by the Brigands (French slaves freed by the leaders of the French revolution) in 1795 but retaken in 1798 by the British. Used as a quarantine centre from 1842 it was abandoned in 1904, became a US observation post during the Second World War and finally the home of Josset Agnes Huchinson, a member of the D'Oyly Carte Theatre who leased it from 1937 to 1976. The bay was then a busy yacht haven and 'Joss' held large parties to entertain the crews. Her abandoned house can still be seen on the south shore of the island.

On the lower of the two peaks lies **Fort Rodney**. The museum (located in the Officers' Mess and rebuilt to the original design) contains a display of the work of the National Trust. None of the interactive displays now works and there is no longer a guide to keep an eye on things. There are two small beaches on Pigeon Island itself, which you can get to by water taxi from Rodney Bay if you don't have a car.

## The north and northeast coasts

*The road north passes through the Cap Estate to Pointe du Cap, a viewpoint some 143 m (470 ft) high with a splendid panorama along the coast. This is the driest part of the island but that hasn't prevented the construction of a good **golf course**, open to visitors. Club St Lucia dominates the hotel scene here and right beside the hotel is **Smugglers' Cove**, a tiny bay reached by descending many steps, which is a good snorkelling spot. On the northeast coast are some* *spectacular and rather inaccessible beaches, wild and windswept and traditional nesting places for leatherback turtles. Most of these are unsafe for swimming, but **Cas-en-Bas** in the north is very protected in a secluded bay. **Turtle watching** takes place at **Grande Anse**, a huge expanse of sand on the Atlantic coast.*

▸▸ *See Sleeping p100, Eating and drinking p120*

---

*If exploring the Atlantic beaches by vehicle, make sure it is a 4WD, check your spare tyre and tools, take OS map and water, be prepared to park and walk, and if possible take a local person with you. Always take local advice on the state of the roads, which change quickly.*

---

## ◉ Sights

---

### Cas-en-Bas and Atlantic beaches in the northeast
*A 45-min walk or arrange a taxi from Gros Islet.  Map 1, A5, p204*

**Cas-en-Bas Beach** is sheltered, shady and a bit dirty, but challenging for experienced windsurfers. *Marjorie's Beach Bar,* **T** 4508637, can organize hikes and horse riding finishing with a meal at the restaurant. The bay is shallow and protected by offshore reefs and usually very calm. Seaweed can occasionally be a problem. The Admiral Estates development on the right as you approach the beach is well underway. **Donkey Beach** can be reached by taking a track to the north (20 minutes' walk); the scenery is wild and open and it is windy.

● *A good circular walk from Gros Islet can be done to Cas-en-Bas taking the road past La Panache Guesthouse (ask the owner, Henry Augustin for directions if necessary, he is always willing to help) down to the beach, then following tracks north until you reach the golf course, from where you return along the west coast to Gros Islet. You will see cacti, wild scenery, Martinique and no tourists.*

To the south of Cas-en-Bas Beach are **Anse Lavoutte**, **Anse Comerette** and **Anse Lapins**: follow the rocks, it is a 30-minute walk to the first and an hour to the last. Access is also possible from Monchy (but only over private property). They are deserted, windswept beaches and headlands.

The road to Monchy from Gros Islet is a pleasant drive inland through several small villages.

### Dauphin Beach
*The beach can be reached from Monchy (reasonable with jeep).*
*Map 1, B7, p204*

There are Indian stone carvings on Dauphin Beach. Once on the beach, wade across the river and walk back in the flat, clear area below the bush land. After about 50 m you'll find long stones with regular depressions. Another 20 m or so and you'll reach a stone pillar about which Robert Devaux wrote: "The carving appears to be a family of three – male, female and child. It is finely executed and must have taken some prehistoric 'Michelangelo' a considerable time to complete the carving." (from *St Lucia Historic Sites*, St Lucia National Trust, 1975, highly recommended, in the library at the Folk Research Centre). It is now used as the St Lucia National Trust's logo. Unfortunately the stone pillar has been badly tampered with. A few metres further inland is the ruin of a colonial church tower, destroyed in 1795 during the French Revolution of St Lucia together with the rest of the settlement.

### Inland route from Monchy to Babonneau and around
*Map 1, p204*

Heading south from Monchy, you gradually leave the dry north part of the island and climb into forest. The ridge between Mount Monier and Mount Chaubourg gives particularly impressive views over the east coast. There are no road signs. Watch out for the names on schools and if in doubt at junctions bear west. At the larger village of Babonneau, you can turn right to follow the river down to the northwest coast at Choc Bay or go straight on to Fond Cacao where a west turn will take you back to Castries and an east turn towards Fond Assor home of the touristy **Fond Latislab Creole Park** (Fond Assor, Babonneau. Book through *Heritage Tours*, La Place Carenage and Pointe Seraphine, **T** 4516058). Visitors come here on organized tours to see demonstrations of Creole skills and traditions. You can see people making cassava bread, cooking on macambou leaves, collecting honey from a hive or sawing wood to the music of a chak chak band.

## Grande Anse

*Currently not open to the general public although turtle watching is organized, Mon-Sat, Mar-Jul. Access is from the village of Desbarra via the private Grande Anse Estate.  Map 1, C7, p204 See also Kids p167*

Back on the east coast, Grande Anse, is a long windy beach and one of the most important nesting sites in the Caribbean for the leatherback turtle see p54. From honeymooners to retirees, tourists and St Lucians all hope for a memorable experience counting the leathery eggs as they drop when the sea turtle comes ashore, oblivious to all.

Visits to Grand Anse to see the turtles can only be done in organized groups and from March to July. The Desbarra community conducts tours with 14 trained guides available. Contact *Heritage Tours*, **T** 4516058/4581726, info@heritagetoursstlucia.com, *Moses Wilfred*, **T** 4506080 or the *Turtle Watch* hotline, **T** 4523224 for information and reservations. Hotel transfers, evening meal and breakfast are part of the EC$120 package: set off at 1600, return around 0700; take food, drink, torch, insect repellent, good walking shoes and warm clothing; tents are supplied. Be prepared for wind, rain or perfect nights. Children are welcome.

## Turtles at Grand Anse

A massive turtle slips from the ocean waves and pauses on the edge of the surf. All is quiet. In the light of the moon, she hauls her heavy body further up the beach. A cluster of people stand motionless and nearly breathless, fearful that the giant sea turtle will sense them and return to the ocean without laying her eggs.

The leatherback turtle (*Demochelys coriacea*) roams the open oceans, feeding on a diet of jellyfish, including the deadly Portuguese man-of-war, which is why the meat of the leatherback is not usually eaten as it can be toxic. Sea turtles swim with grace and speed and have been clocked at an amazing 22 miles per hour.

Leatherback turtles here weigh around 800-1,000 lbs, but male leatherbacks can reach a length of 2.5 m (8 ft) and weigh up to 2,000 lbs. Only a mature female comes ashore and then only to make a nest and lay 60-120 eggs, perhaps several times in one season but only every two to three years. Leatherbacks require sandy nesting beaches backed with vegetation and sloped sufficiently so that the crawl to dry sand is not too far. A suitable depth of coarse, dry sand is important, because the female first excavates a pit for her body and then must reach moist sand before she can make the proper flask-shaped nest. Incubation takes from 55 to 74 days and emergence of the hatchlings occurs at night. The turtles are believed to reach maturity in six to 10 years and may live to the grand age of 80.

Hawksbill and Green turtles also come ashore here but not so often.

All sea turtles are endangered. Sand mining, construction close to the water, human and other animal and bird predators, destroy habitats. Their diet is one reason why they frequently fall prey to marine pollution, eating plastic bags because they look like jellyfish.

## Anse Louvet

*3 hours' walk but not drivable from Desbarra, 2 hours' walk, or drive if possible, from Aux Leon; the steep track is impassable on a wet day. Anse Louvet Estate is private, so technically you have to trespass to get to the public beach.  Map 1, E7, p204*

Anse Louvet is a sheltered beach in a stunning setting with a special, spooky atmosphere but swimming is not recommended on these Atlantic beaches. Ask locally about the erratic state of the roads. Walking takes as long as driving; take lots of water. La Sorcière mountain forms a long wall which seems to separate Louvet from the rest of the world. Rugged cliffs are beaten by waves and there is a blow hole. A high waterfall in the forest can be reached by following the river from the ford in the main valley (little water flow).

# East coast to Vieux Fort

*The southeastern seaboard is a mass of fjords, spiky peninsulas and squiggly bays. Communities on this side of the island grew up wherever there was a fresh water supply and they made their living from fishing. **Dennery** is still a fishing village of some importance, although there is little for the visitor to see. There are several nature reserves, from **Fregate Island** down to the **Maria Islands**, which protect endangered species, and **Mamiku Gardens**, a fine example of a tropical cultivated garden. There are plenty of **hiking** opportunities from the relatively easy **East Coast Trail**, to the **Des Cartiers Rainforest Trail** which can take you across the whole island. In the far south is **Vieux Fort**, an industrial town and site of the international airport. At the tip of the island is an old light house, with amazing views looking back up the island to the mountains. The long, sandy beach of Anse de Sables is great for **windsurfing** and **kiteboarding**, as well as swimming, with strong, onshore winds.*

▶▶ *See Sleeping p100, Eating and drinking p120*

The new road from Castries to Cul de Sac, known as the Millennium Highway, was immediately popular with cars and trucks. It is quite a straight road running along the sea and is a welcome relief from the hairpin curves of the old Morne Road. The Castries end starts at the roundabout on La Toc Road, goes through two short tunnels and comes out in the Cul de Sac valley, where a right turn takes you towards the beautiful Marigot Bay and the West Coast Road to Vieux Fort. A jog to the left and then a quick right takes the East Coast Road to the southern end of the island. The West Coast Road is full of mountain curves but has less traffic than the East Coast. Together they present a very scenic drive round the island.

The transinsular road goes through extensive banana plantations with the occasional packaging plant, through the village of Ravine Poisson before climbing steeply over the Barre de l'Isle ridge, the mountain barrier that divides the island. As you come out of the rainforest and approach the east coast there are spectacular views down to the  Atlantic coast.

#  Sights

### Barre de l'Isle Rainforest Trail

Forestry Department, Union, **T** 4502231 Ext 316, forestrails@ slumaffe.org  *Guides available Mon-Fri, 0830-1500. Pay on site, US$10. Guides arranged at weekends cost more. 30 mins' drive from Castries. Access from main road, parking by a snack bar where guides wait. Bus 2B or 2C from Castries.  Map 1, F5, p204  See also Kids p167*

There is a short, circular trail at the high point on the road between Castries and Dennery, which takes about 10 minutes and affords good views of the rainforest and down the Roseau valley. You walk through dense forest with some pine trees.The path is good, single file only and there is a small picnic shelter and toilet at

## ▶ Head of the dog - the boa constrictor

This is the largest of the four snakes found on the island, the others being the poisonous fer-de-lance, the Maria Island grass snake and the tiny, blind worm snake.

The boa, also called *tèt-chyen*, grows up to 4 m (about 14 ft) long and lives on small prey which it suffocates in its coils.

In the wild boas live in the drier areas of the island and can often be seen asleep in trees. There are a couple kept at Union zoo and you sometimes see men displaying them at the roadside as a tourist attraction.

240 m (800 ft) with a view down to the Caribbean. A boa constrictor can often be found sleeping in a tree nearby. It can be slippery after rain but it is not steep. The experience is rather spoilt by the noise of traffic. However, the main trail is about a mile long and takes an hour, coming back on the same path. There are several lookout points from where you can see Morne Gimie, the Cul-de-Sac valley on the west and the Mabouya valley and Fond d'Or on the east. On the trail you may see the St Lucia parrot as well as many other birds such as the St Lucia oreole, St Lucia warbler, thrashers and pewees while mongoose and agouti also live in the forest. A longer steeper walk to the top of Mount La Combe from the end of this trail takes another hour.

For an even longer hike (guide essential) you can take a rugged 11-mile trail which will eventually bring you out on the Des Cartiers Trail (see p63), but this can take anything up to 24 hours depending on conditions and your level of fitness.

## Piton Flore

Contact Loretta Robinson, Chairperson for the Forestière Guides Association, **T** 4525092/5842184, or Julia Constantine, **T** 4882871. *EC$10 adults, EC$5 children. Bus 2B or 2C from Castries. 30 mins' drive. Entrance on other side of road from Barre de l'Isle trail by visitor centre and toilets. Map 1, F5, p204*

La Sorcière and Piton Flore are densely forested mountains in the north with excellent rainforest vegetation. Piton Flore is a 5-mile hike from the visitor centre and classified as moderate to strenuous with one steep part. The trail is now a community effort managed in conjunction with *Heritage Tours*. You will need to ask how to get to the top, where the satellite and phone masts are, from where there are spectacular views. It is the last recorded location of Semper's warbler, which hasn't been seen since 1972 and is believed to be extinct.

## Fond d'Or Nature and Historical Park

Mabouya Valley Development Programme, Mabouya, Dennery, **T** 4533242. Heritage Tours, La Place Carenage and Pointe Seraphine, **T** 4516058, www.heritagetoursstlucia.com *Free entry. Creole food and restrooms available. Map 1, F7, p204*

The park is in the beautiful Mabouya valley in the Dennery basin and is being managed as a Heritage Tourism site. As you look down to the Atlantic ocean you'll see some large rocks at the head of the bay. Because of their shape, carved by the waves, they are known as the Mabouya Man and his sleeping lion. The man appears to have his mouth open while the lion is reclining. Amerindian settlers regarded them as gods.

**!** The name Mabouya comes from 'Ma Boyé' which means 'without beginning' and is closely associated with the snake. There are indeed boa constrictors in Fond d'Or park.

Mabouya was believed to be a mischievous spirit needing constant reverence to prevent him bringing misfortune on man. Children still fear the Mabouya, who figures in scary tales.

The Mabouya valley is the largest on the east coast and in colonial times was a centre for sugar cane, rum and slaves. There are ruins of sugar mills in the park as well as an Amerindian site, mangrove and estuarine forest, trails through dry scrub woodland to a sandy beach (swimming is dangerous) where leatherback turtles come to nest, and a new campsite. Fond d'Or is now closely associated with the annual Jazz Festival, hosting some of the leading events, and is a popular site for family picnics.

## Dennery and around
*Bus 2C from Castries. 45 mins' drive.*   Map 1, F7, p204

The road descends through Grande Rivière to Dennery where the vegetation is mostly xerophytic scrub. Dennery is set in a sheltered bay with Dennery Island guarding its entrance. As you come into town notice the new fire station beside the road on the hill, with what has to be the best view for any fire station in the world across dramatic bays with rocks, islets and promontories. The village below is dominated by the Roman Catholic **church**. Here you can see the distinctive **St Lucia fishing boats** pulled up on the beach. Carved out of single tree trunks, the bows are straight and pointed rather than curved and are all named with phrases such as 'God help me'. A US$6 million **fishing port** has been built with improved moorings and cold storage, with Japanese assistance. There are lots of small bars but no other facilities. At the weekend, however, the town invites visitors to a **fish fest**, when from 1600-0200, you can join in a street party, eat freshly caught and cooked seafood and enjoy music and dancing, if you feel the urge. You can follow the Dennery River west and inland towards Mount Beaujolais and the **Errard Plantation**, often included in organized tours of the east coast, where there are waterfalls and you can see nutmeg and cocoa grown and processed. Up on the hill just after Dennery to the south is the island's new prison, Bordelais, a 'correctional facility', which like the fire station, enjoys a spectacular outlook.

## Eastern Nature Trail and Praslin Island

Heritage Tours, **T** 4516058, heritagetours@candw.lc   *Minimum 4 people US$12 per person, including tour guide, single entry is US$5 with an additional US$25 for the guide. Option of Praslin Island for US$8 more. Bus 2H or 2I from Castries.   Map 1, F-G7, p204*

Just after Dennery you will see a sign for the Eastern Nature Trail, which winds its way along the coast between the road and the sea for 3 ½ miles from Mandele to Praslin Bay, with exit points every mile, so you can stop when you want to. You walk through fields, forests, up cliffs and down to the beach. You do not have to have a guide on the trail, although they will point out the names and uses of all the plants and wildlife you might otherwise miss, but you will only be allowed on Praslin Island on an organized tour. **Praslin Island**, in the bay, is one of only two islands where St Lucian whiptails live. They used to live only on Maria Major Island until being successfully introduced here to prevent annihilation by hurricanes or any other natural disaster.

## Fregate Island Nature Reserve

National Trust, **T** 4525005, natrust@candw.lc   *Entry by prior reservation only, US$20 with guide, US$5 without, US$2.50 children. Map 1, G7, p205*

The Fregate Islands, on the north side of Praslin Bay are two small islands, nesting sites from May to July for the frigate bird. The larger island rises sheer out of the sea and was clearly once joined to the mainland. You can't actually get to them, but the north **promontory of Praslin Bay** gives a good vantage point just across the water. A trail runs down to the shore and back up by another route. You can do it in under an hour if you don't stop much but there are benches for taking in the scenery and a small beach of both black and golden sand to explore. The dry forest harbours the trembler, the St Lucian oriole and the red-necked pigeon or Ramier. The reserve includes a section of mangrove and is the natural habitat of the boa constrictor (*tèt-chyen*) which you can sometimes see sleeping in the big trees at the end of the peninsula. The area is also of some historical interest as there was an Amerindian lookout point in the reserve and it was later the site of a battle between the English and the Brigands. It used to be known as Trois Islet and the nearby Praslin River is still marked as Trois Islet River on maps today. A lone coconut palm growing at the end of the peninsula was planted in memory of a fisherman who drowned in the area but was never found. You can swim in Praslin Bay and you may see traditional fishing boats, carved out of whole gommier trees, moored at the jetty.

---

### Mamiku Gardens: Botanical Gardens and Woodland Walks

Between Praslin and Mon Repos **T** 4528236, www.mamiku.com *Daily 0900-1700. EC$15 for foreigners, EC$10 for locals, there is a snack bar and souvenir shop.  Map 1, G7, p205*

---

The road leaves the coast at the fishing community of Praslin and goes through banana plantations and the villages of Mon Repos and Patience. Between Praslin and Mon Repos are the Mamiku Gardens. The 12-acre estate and **gardens** are fabulous and an army of gardeners keeps them in excellent condition. You can take a guided tour if you wish, but if you prefer to wander around the paths on your own among the frangipani and ginger lilies, the bush medicine garden and the flowering trees, request a map and plant guide. You can do a circular walk, with spurs off to secluded arbours and secret gardens. Every plant is numbered so you can look up its common name, botanical name and family. There is also an interesting list of locally used herbs and their uses.

The estate was owned by Baron de Micoud, when he was Governor of the island for France in the 18th century, but later became a British military post and site of a battle with Brigands (escaped or freed slaves and French soldiers, see p83). There is an on-going **excavation** at Mamiku which is producing interesting finds from the ruins of the house where the British soldiers were surprised and massacred by the Brigands. For those interested in the history, *Mamiku: The Tale of an 18th Century Sugar Plantation in St Lucia* by Louise Singleton Smith, a member of the family which has owned the estate since 1906, is available in the shop.

● *Down the road, Mon Repos is a good place to see the flower festivals of La Rose in August and La Marguerite in October, see p137.*

## Micoud
*Map 1, I7, p205*

The coast is regained at Micoud but the main road bypasses the town: a mixture of old wooden houses and modern concrete buildings. There are one or two restaurants, a department store, post office and a branch of FirstCaribbean International bank. They make **wine** here: banana, guava, pineapple and sugar cane brewed and bottled under Helen Brand and available in some supermarkets. Their ginger wine is recommended, light, not too sweet, with just the right amount of 'bite'. One mile west of Micoud is **Latille Gardens** with fruit, flowers, trees and waterfalls. From Mahaut Road follow signs to the south. Tours can also be arranged through hotels and include a walk through the Des Cartiers Rainforest Trail, **T** 4540202.

**!** The St Lucia parrot became endangered for many reasons but one old story said that if you ate the parrot's head you would speak more fluently, so hunters killed and ate them.

> ### Endangered parrot

Known locally as the *jacquot*, the St Lucia parrot (*Amazona versicolor*) is a very colourful bird with a green body, blue crown, turquoise cheeks, a touch of maroon on the under parts, red on the foreneck and a red patch on the wing.

A seriously endangered species a few years ago because of hunting, both for food and the pet trade, and competition from other birds for habitat – many of the parrots' nesting sites were destroyed by hurricanes – and their population faced extinction in the 1970s. A concerted effort to save them through protection, education and breeding has now raised the numbers to over 800 in the wild.

They are best seen in the mountains around Quillesse, Edmond Forest and Millet.

---

### Des Cartiers Rainforest Trail

6 miles west of Mahaut, signed from main road. Forestry Department, Union, **T** 4502231 Ext 316, forestrails@slumaffe.org *Guides available Mon-Fri, 0830-1500. Pay on site, US$10. Guides can be arranged at weekends but will cost more. No buses from main road. Taxis from Castries about US$50. Best to hire a car or book a tour.* Map 1, H/I 15, p205

---

The trail through the rainforest is a loop of about 2 ½ miles taking around two hours. You have to look where you are putting your feet and it can be slippery, but there are no steep climbs and Forestry classifies it as easy to moderate. It starts from the rangers' station, where there are extremely basic toilets and seating for briefing talks, but not much else. The rainforest here is thick and lush and it is perfect for birdwatching, with many of the endemics found here. You can stay over night by prior arrangement at a very basic lodge called La Porte, which would allow you to be in the right place early in the morning for parrot watching. It is extremely basic, bunk beds,no electricity, mosquitoes, an outside and inside shower and toilet, an outdoor kitchen with coal pots and a barbeque, picnic tables and a camping area for tents. There is a track to the lodge, so vehicles can reach it. A ranger will stay overnight with you if you have arranged a guide. For serious hikers you can walk to the furthest point and then continue to the Edmond Forest Reserve, thereby crossing the island. Ask the Forestry Department about doing this.

### Savannes Bay Nature Reserve
*Bus route 2H or 2I from Castries. Turn off the road at the sign to Mankote Mangrove to get to the beach.  Map 1, K6, p205*

Mangrove swamps can be seen at Savannes Bay Nature Reserve. The shallow bay is protected by a reef and is excellent for the cultivation of sea moss, an ideal breeding ground for conch and sea eggs. Scorpion Island lies in the bay and to the north are more archaeological sites on Saltibus Point and Pointe de Caille. There are kayaking tours you can go on through the mangroves (booked through hotels) or you can hire a boat from Anse de Sables for a ride along the coast, pulling in to see the sea moss farms. The boats going to the Maria Islands will often deviate to take you there if you ask. Sea moss is grown on ropes suspended just below the surface of the sea by hundreds of plastic bottles as buoys.

### Vieux Fort
*Bus 2H or 2I from Castries. The bus terminal is at the end of Clarke Street near the airport (see p21).  Map 1, L5-6, p205*

Vieux Fort is the island's industrial centre, with a Free Zone and the Hewanorra International Airport. It is an active town with a good Saturday market and a lot of traditional housing; open-topped, gaily painted trucks are still used on special occasions. The area is

**Somewhere over the rainbow**
*Coconut palm-forested hills watch over St Lucia's picture-perfect views.*

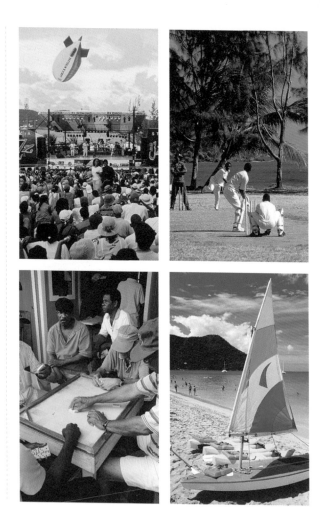

1  The annual St Lucia Jazz Festival in May draws enthusiastic crowds in their thousands. Most concerts are open air and it's not just jazz: your feet will be moving to Latin, salsa, soca, reggae, zouk and more.
▶▶ See page 139.

2  Gearing up for the Cricket World Cup in 2007, St Lucia will be hosting the England team matches.
▶▶ See page 153.

3  Daily life in Laborie, where wooden chattel houses are home to many generations of the same family.
▶▶ See page 14.

4  The serious game of dominoes played in Castries, the capital of St Lucia. ▶▶ See page 35.

5  Reduit beach on Rodney bay is an excellent base for watersports, close to the Rodney Bay Marina.
▶▶ See page 48.

6  St Lucia's drive-in volcano, hot mud pools at the Sulphur Springs, Soufrière.
▶▶ See page 80.

**Faded glory**
*Balenbouche Estate, formerly a sugar plantation, is still a working farm today, producing fruit for local markets.*

**Lobster quadrille**
*Fishing villages serve up freshly caught and cooked seafood to all-comers as a special Friday night treat.*

**Mango walk**
*Bag some fresh local fruit on market day in Anse La Raye.*

**Calypso beat**
*The carnival in July will test your party stamina with hours of music, dancing and drinking.*

**Action man**
Trails through the forest are ideal for hiking or biking, an adrenaline-fuelled antidote to lazing on the beach.

## The first tourists

The first Amerindians to make the migration from the Orinoco and the northern coast of the Guianas arrived in St Lucia around AD200, somewhat later than in the other islands of the Lesser Antilles. It is not known whether they bypassed St Lucia during earlier migrations or whether indeed they landed and their settlements are yet to be discovered by archaeologists. Remnants of the first settlers to arrive by canoe have been found at Grande Anse on the east coast and at Anse Noir in the south near Vieux Fort. They are now referred to as Island Arawaks, although Arawak refers to a language rather than a people.

There is abundant evidence that the Island Arawaks farmed the fertile soils of the interior and their pottery has been found scattered over large areas in Saltibus and Parc Estate. When they were too far from the coast to live on fish, they ate iguanas, crabs, crawfish and other animals. They stayed on St Lucia until around 1450, when they were replaced by the Caribs. No one yet knows what happened, whether they were killed, or driven out, but the pottery made by the Island Arawaks ceased to be made after that date and when the first European settlers arrived at the beginning of the 16th century, there were only Caribs in residence. Caribs survived here until the late 17th century but were then sent off to St Vincent and thence to Central America. Nowadays only a small community survives on Dominica.

markedly less sophisticated than the north of the island. The town boasts two new supermarkets in malls, *JQs* and *Julian's*. The latter has a cinema. The police station and post office, on Theodore Street, are right in the middle of the town. Fishing boats are pulled up on the small strand but there is no proper beach here. On

**Clarke Street** you will pass shops and colonial-style homes and the square with a war memorial and bandstand.

There is plenty of evidence that the Island Arawaks had many settlements in the southern part of the island and cultivated crops on the relatively flat land in the foothills of the central mountains. Archaeologists have found remains of houses and petroglyphs all round the coast. It is believed that the Dutch were the first Europeans to try and settle the south, setting up a short-lived base at Vieux Fort around 1600. It later became an important area for sugar cane, with both the French and the British working plantations with slave labour. In World War II, the Americans built an airbase here which has now become the island's main international airport. The USA received 3,000 acres of land at Vieux Fort and 120 acres at Gros Islet as part of a package of bases in the Caribbean, Bermuda and Newfoundland in return for 50 reconditioned destroyers. St Lucians were delighted at the prospect of paid jobs and a market for their produce. This era of prosperity became known as *An tan Laméwichains* (at the time of the Americans), and rum shops, night clubs and dance halls sprung up and flourished. However, there were structural problems: in 1942 there were 8,000 people from many islands living here but only 300 houses for them to live in. Sanitation left a lot to be desired. Typhoid, tuberculosis and venereal disease increased, but so did people's incomes, allowing them to buy clothes, shoes and better food. The US military drained most of the mangrove swamps around Vieux Fort, thereby getting rid of malaria. Both bases were dismantled in 1949, but by that time a lot of the migrant workers had already moved on.

## Anse de Sables
Vieux Fort. *Bus 2H or 2I from Castries.*   Map 1, L6, p205

Also known as Sandy Beach, this is the longest stretch of golden sand beach on the island. You can walk for miles along adjoining beaches and hardly see a soul. There used to be a *Club Med* resort here, but it is now closed. Sandals is planning to build a *Beaches* family resort instead, possibly opening in 2005, but for the time being it is free of mass tourism and you can spend a peacful day swimming and sunbathing. On the main part of the beach you can find beach bars, a *Mistral* windsurfing school and *Tornado* windsurfing and kitesurfing school (see sports, p160). January and February are the best months for wind but May is also good. From mid June to the end of October the winds are unreliable because of the hurricane season and the schools close for the summer.

● *Note that apart from a few sea grapes there is no shade on the beach.*

## Maria Islands

The National Trust, head office, **T** 4525005, Southern Regional office **T** 4545014, natrust@candw.lc  *US$35/EC$94 per person for 2 people for boat and guide, less for larger groups. By reservation only. Unauthorized access is not allowed. The package of transport, tour, lunch for min 4 people is US$75 per person.  Map1, L6, p205*

The airport perimeter road skirts Anse de Sables beach, and looks across to the Maria Islands: Maria Major (25 acres), which you can visit, and Maria Minor (4 acres), which is just a rocky outcrop once overgrazed by goats and now left alone. A trip to the islands is well worth doing as you get a combination of nature tour, boat ride and beach, all in a spectacular setting with tremendous views over St Lucia. The Maria Islands are home to two endemic reptiles, a colourful lizard and a small, very rare, harmless grass snake, the St Lucia racer, also known as the *kouwès* or couresse snake. The lizard, *Cnemidophorus vanzoi*, is known as *zandoli tè* in Kwéyòl and lives only here and on Praslin Island, where it was introduced to protect numbers. The males, about 18 cm long, sport the colours of the national flag. The females are brown with some white spots along their belly. You will hear them scuttling under bushes so keep your ears and eyes peeled. There are several other lizards on the island, including the rock gecko which hides in cracks in the rocks. The couresse snake can often be found in the hollow of a forked tree where a pool of water has collected as it likes to keep damp and cool. The guide will point it out to you if it is at home. The Maria Islands are also a nesting site for many seabirds, the ground dove and red-necked pigeon, among others. From May to July public access is restricted while the birds are nesting in their hundreds on the cliffs and on the ground. This means that you can not do the whole tour and can only go as far as a viewpoint by which time the terns will be wheeling round your head in protest. At other times of the year you can walk to the cliff top at the end of the island and see the rock face where the terns, boobies, noddies, frigate birds and tropic birds make their home.

The interpretative centre on Anse de Sables beach is not always open as the National Trust guide only comes if she has a tour. When you book a tour with the National Trust, your guide will take you further up Anse de Sables to the restaurant *Chak Chak*, from where the boats go across to the island. You will be given life jackets for the crossing. Take walking shoes as flip flops aren't great for the rocky parts of the trail and there are cactus spines. Be prepared to get wet getting into the boat as there is no jetty. There is a nice beach on the leeward side of Maria Major facing back to Anse de Sables and the snorkelling is good, so take your mask and fins. If you go on a tour with an agency they will provide gear but the National Trust does not.

## Cap Moule à Chique
*Map 1, L6, p205*

This is the most southerly point on the island and from the lighthouse or the masts you get a spectacular view of the whole of the south of St Lucia with all its mountains. Turn left at the T junction and follow the road to the banana loading jetty (on

Wednesday you will pass truck after truck waiting to be weighed).
Bear left and go up a badly maintained track. Finally go left again
through the Cable and Wireless site up to the **lighthouse**. The
duty officer will be glad to point out the views including the Pitons,
Morne Gomier (313 m,1028 ft) with Morne Grand Magazin (616 m,
2022 ft) behind it. Unfortunately Morne Gimie (950 m, 3118 ft) is
largely obscured. Further to the east is Piton St Esprit (585 m, 1919
ft) and Morne Durocher (322 m,1055 ft) near Praslin. The
lighthouse itself is 223 m (730 ft) above sea level and also has good
views over the Maria islands and southwest to St Vincent.

## West Coast to Soufrière and the Pitons

*The west coast has some of the most stunning and beautiful scenery
in the Caribbean, principally around the **Pitons**, green volcanic cones
whose slopes plunge dramatically into the sea and provide endless
photo shoots for travel brochures. In June 2004 they were declared a
UNESCO World Heritage Site, and the Pitons Management Area
includes Gros Piton, Petit Piton, the town of Soufrière, the sulphur
springs, the coral reefs and all the fauna and flora living in the area.
The natural harbour of **Marigot** is picture-book pretty and the
**Roseau valley** around it is one of the main banana growing areas.
**Anse la Raye** is a small fishing village notable for its Friday fish fry,
while inland, **Millet** is one of the best birdwatching places, in the
forests and fields around the Roseau dam. **Soufrière**, once the capital
of the island, is a typically West Indian town of old wooden houses set
on the beautiful bay at the foot of Petit Piton. Offshore is the **marine
park**, providing an underwater safe haven for sea creatures and
some excellent snorkelling and diving. The **Edmond Forest Reserve**
can be reached from here for some excellent forest walking in the
mountains, but most impressive of all are the Soufrière **sulphur
springs** in a volcanic crater referred to as the world's only drive-in
volcano. Further south, the terrain becomes less mountainous and
more agricultural as you head round the south coast via a few fishing*

*villages to Vieux Fort. The lush plantation at **Balenbouche** is known for its Amerindian petroglyphs and other artefacts as well as being a venue for the Jazz Festival.*

▸▸ *See Sleeping p102, Eating and drinking p122, Bars and clubs p130*

*The West Coast Road is in excellent condition with good signposting. It is a curvy, but spectacular, drive down to Soufrière. Take the millennium highway out of Castries and instead of branching left at Cul de Sac bay carry straight on. The road quickly rises to La Croix Maingot with good views of the Roseau banana plantation.*

 Sights

## Marigot Bay

*Signposted from the Roseau valley. Bus 3C or 3D from Castries. Map 1, E3, p204*

On reaching the Roseau valley, take the road to Marigot Bay, a beautiful inlet and natural harbour called Hurricane Hole which many years ago provided the setting for the original 1967 film of *Dr Doolittle*. A viewpoint at the top of the hill is a magnet for sellers of souvenirs but it is a pretty view down to the bay. It supports a large marina and not surprisingly a large number of yachts in transit berth here to restock with supplies from the supermarket and chandler. There is a police station and immigration post at the end of the road on the waterfront, as well as bars, disco, restaurants and hotels and guest houses popular with the yachting fraternity. In 2004 there was a lot of construction work with apartments and a hotel being built and the bay was no longer quite the peaceful place it used to be.

The **Marigot Bay Marine Reserve** supports the largest mangrove system on the west coast and includes mangroves and fringing reefs to both the north and south entrance to the bay. You will notice a small strip of land jutting out into the bay. This has a little beach (not particularly good for swimming) and can be reached by the *Gingerbread Express* (a water taxi, EC$2 return, refundable at *Doolittle's* restaurant if you eat or drink there), either from the hotel or from the customs post. It is a good place for arranging watersports.

## Roseau Valley

The Roseau valley is the principal banana growing area on the island and everywhere you look there are bananas. The valley is prone to mudslides and flooding during storms, which periodically wipe out the whole crop. It used to be a big sugar-growing area and for that reason there is a **rum distillery** here. *St Lucia Distillers* have excellent tours of the factory and you can taste and buy their produce, see p31. At **Jacmel**, a village in the valley just off the West Coast Road, the church has murals of the black madonna painted by Dunstan St Omer see p187.

## Millet Bird Sanctuary Trail

Forestry Department, **T** 4511691, forestrails@slumaffe.org *Open Mon-Fri 0830-1500, US$10. Weekends by prior arrangement with higher prices. Birdwatching tours by reservation 24 hours in advance, US$30, starting early in the morning and lasting over 4 hours. 45 mins from Castries turning left opposite the turning to the rum distillery and then right at Vanard, or by going to Anse la Raye and turning left as you get through the village on the road past La Sikwi. Bus route 3B from Castries to Millet. Map 1 E3, p204*

This area of secondary rainforest in the heart of the island at 1,000 ft above sea level is one of the best places for birdwatching. The land has recently been acquired by the Forestry Department to protect the Roseau Dam on the property and its watershed, with farmers being given land elsewhere. There is a high biodiversity

▶ **Forest birds of St Lucia**

**St Lucia oriole**  *carouge* (*Icterus laudabilis*)
Measuring 20-22 cm, mostly black with orange patches on the upper wing-coverts, under wing-coverts, rump, abdomen, flanks and under tail-coverts.

**Blue hooded euphonia**  *perruche, jacquot carim* (*Euphonia musica*) 12 cm long with a yellow forehead and blue head while the body is mostly green above and yellowish green underneath.

**St Lucia warbler**  *sikwi barbade, petit chit*
Formerly Adelaide's warbler (*Dendroica adelaidae*) but reclassified because it has black round the eyes, not white. The upper parts are grey and the under parts bright yellow.

**Purple throated carib**  *kilibri rouge*  (*Eulampis jugularis*)
A sturdy 13-cm hummingbird with dark plumage and purplish red throat but noticeable for its metallic green wings.

**Semper's warbler**  *pied blanc* (*Leucopeza semperi*)
Last seen in 1972 at Piton Flore, it has dark grey upper parts and whitish under parts and measures 15 cm.

**St Lucia black finch**  *moisson; pyé blan*
(*Melanospiza richardsoni*)  13-14 cm, the male is black with pink feet, the female is greyer.

with many fruit trees as well as forest and over 30 species of birds can be found here, including five endemics: the St Lucia parrot, St Lucia black finch, St Lucia oriole, St Lucia pewee and St Lucia warbler. The well-maintained, 1¾-mile loop trail takes about two hours to walk with only one steep section up to a panoramic view of Morne Gimie, the forest and Roseau Dam, the largest stretch of water in the Eastern Caribbean. If you want to see parrots it is best to arrange a tour at dawn, but you can see birds at any time of day.

**Trembler** *twanblè* (*Cinclocerthia ruficauda*)
A dark brown to olive grey bird measuring 23-25 cm with greyish white under parts and a long, slender bill. It really does tremble.

**Rufous-throated solitaire** *siffleur montagne* (*Myadestes genibarbis*) Mostly grey, about 19 cm, with a rufous throat, foreneck and posterior underparts.

**Pearly-eyed thrasher** *gwo grieve* (*Margarops fuscatus*) Rather like a thrush, the 28-cm thrasher has a heavy brownish yellow bill, its upper parts are dark greyish brown and its under parts are white with greyish brown markings.

**St Lucia pewee** *pin caca* Formerly Lesser Antillean pewee (*Contopus latirostris*) but reclassified because of colour differences. A flycatcher about 17 cm with rufous coloured underparts and olive grey upper parts.

See also **St Lucia parrot** p63

## Anse La Raye
*On the main road to Soufrière. Bus route 3C or 3D.* Map 1, F2, p204

The fishing villages of Anse La Raye has become famous for its **fish fry** on Front Street, the seafront road, on Fridays which attracts hundreds of people to eat lobster in season and fish and seafood at any time of year, freshly caught and cooked at stalls along the street (see p122). It is also a popular stop on a tour of this coast, with the street lined with souvenir stalls during the day. When you turn down into the village from the main road, stop just before you get to Front Street and on your right you will see a small **bakery** still using the traditional oven. You can buy delicious hot turnovers, a sweet bread roll stuffed with coconut and sugar, for a tourist price of US$1 (only EC$1 in the supermarkets). The village of old wooden cottages, many of them with attractive decorative details and verandas, also has a large and simple Roman Catholic church, the Church of the Nativity of the Blessed Virgin Mary.

### La Sikwi

**T** 4526323 in Castries, **T** 4514245 at the mill to arrange a visit and tour. *To the south of Anse La Raye, take the last road to the left before you reach the bridge up past the school* Map 1, F2, p204

South of Anse La Raye, La Sikwi is a well-restored **sugar mill,** and can be visited by prior arrangement. It is beside the river where women still come to wash their laundry, on the way to a waterfall. The gardens are very colourful and beautiful, with paths winding through the many flowering plants. Boa constrictor come here to be fed and with luck you will see one. Inside the mill there are many items from the sugar-making process on display and everything is well laid out. The bar and restaurant open on demand and are used mostly for tour parties. Behind the mill there is a stage, used occasionally for shows and events.

### Anse Cochon

*It is accessed from Ti Kaye Hotel whose drive is signed on a very sharp bend in the main road after you have ascended from Anse La Raye.* Map 1, F2, p204

Anse Cochon is a perfect sweep of dark golden sand in a small bay at the bottom of cliffs, part of the Canaries/Anse La Raye Marine Management Area (CAMMA). From the *Ti Kaye Hotel*, see p103, you go down 169 steps to the beach, bar, dive shop and sea. Guests at the hotel use it and it is a customary stop over for tour boats returning from Soufrière, so it can get crowded in the afternoon, but otherwise it is quiet and secluded. Diving is good here as there is a wreck just offshore, and snorkelling gear can be hired from the beach bar for around US$10 a day.

### Anse Jambette and Canaries

*A narrow, steep, bad road branches off to the right just before Canaries and leads to a former restaurant at Anse Jambette.*
*Map 1, G2, p205*

The bay and the beach are worth visiting and snorkelling is quite good here. Half way along this road, before it gets really steep, you can park and climb down the hill towards Canaries. There is a man-made cave and oven once used by escaped slaves. Difficult to find (as intended), you need a knowledgeable local to show you where it is. There are many waterfalls in the vicinity of Canaries, some of which are visited by organized tours. If you go independently you need a 4WD and a guide. Ask in the village or at *Ti Kaye* hotel. The closest is right at the end of the road into the rainforest, others are 30 minutes to 2½ hours walk away. It is safe to swim. The village of Canaries has little to offer the visitor, but it is interesting to see the traditional wooden houses and the laundry being done in the river with sheets spread out on the stones.

### Anse La Liberté

South of Canaries. National Trust, **T** 4537656, www.slunatrust.org
*Water taxi from Canaries, EC$2. Map 1, G2, p205*

Anse La Liberté is a National Trust site and a hiking and camping site (see p107) on 133 acres spread over the hillside and down to the black sand beach at the bottom. There is a poor road to the office, from where a trail leads to the sea, or you can take the 'short cut'. This is a turning before you get to the sign for the campsite,

★ **Empty beaches**

• Anse La Liberté, p75
• Maria Islands, p67
• Anse Louvet, p55
• Grand Anse, p53
• Anse de Sables, p66

recognized by the red and white barrier. It climbs steeply uphill, initially a concrete track but it soon deteriorates and high clearance or 4WD is necessary. At the end of the road you have to leave your vehicle and walk from the Bro Iyee Hippolyte Community Centre (named after the elderly guardian) along a nature trail (10 minutes down, 15 minutes up) and down a ladder to the beach. Snorkelling is good from the beach but you have to bring your own equipment. It is very quiet and peaceful and you are unlikely to be disturbed. There is a fantastic 180° view of the coast north and south from the Community Centre and it is a wonderful place to watch the sunset. There are many Brigand holes in the area.

### Soufrière
*Bus route 3D from Castries, 2 hours. Few return buses after midday, best to go back via Vieux Fort, changing buses at Vieux Fort cross-roads. Buses to Castries leave from the market area of Soufrière. If you arrive by boat head for the north end of the bay, you will find plenty of help to tie up your yacht (EC$5) and taxis will appear from nowhere. It is a much cheaper alternative to tying up at the jetty. Organized tours available from the hotels further north, by sea or road, from US$65-80 include lunch, drinks, transfers and a trip to Soufrière, Diamond Gardens and the Sulphur Springs (see below). Map 1, I2, p205*

After Canaries the road goes inland and skirts Mount Tabac (678 m, 2,224 ft) before descending into Soufrière. This is the most picturesque and interesting part of the island, with marvellous old wooden buildings at the foot of the spectacular Pitons, now a UNESCO World Heritage Site, surrounded by thick vegetation and towering rock formations looming out of the sea. Because of its location, the town is a must for tourists. Soufrière is a charming old West Indian town dating back to 1713 when Louis XIV of France granted the lands around Soufrière to the three brothers of the Devaux family for their loyalty to the Crown. The estate subsequently produced cotton, tobacco, coffee and cocoa. During the French Revolution, the guillotine was raised in the square by the Brigands but the Devaux family were protected by loyal slaves and escaped.

The **square** nowadays is a quiet and pretty place with lots of old French colonial houses with shutters and overhanging balconies creating shady walkways underneath, all decorated in the gingerbread style with lots of intricate fretwork. Unfortunately many of them are crumbling and haven't had the attention and investment that the old houses around the Derek Walcott Square in Castries have received. The Lady of the Assumption church was built in 1952 and survived a huge fire in 1955, along with all the old houses south of the square. There is a **market** to the north of the harbour, where you can buy straw hats, crafts, spices and coal pots. The fish market is behind the Old Court House restaurant and the fruit and veg market, held on Saturday mornings, is on the waterfront and the streets off it. The population is now around 10,000 and the town is on a very picturesque bay totally dominated by the Pitons. The **waterfront** is the centre of action in the town and the place where most tour parties come in by boat from Castries or Rodney Bay. Sadly they are usually whisked of by coach on a tour of the region with no time to wander the streets of town. The water here is extremely deep and reaches 61 m (200 ft) only a few yards from the shore, which is why boats moor close in. There is a dark sand beach to the north of the bay in front of the *Hummingbird Beach Resort* and lots of colourful wooden fishing boats pulled up on the shore. A conch shell is blown when fish has been landed. For good swimming and snorkelling, however, get a water taxi (quicker and more comfortable than going by road) round the coast to Anse Chastanet. The Soufrière Water Taxi Association sets standard rates for excursions around the coast.

## Anse Chastanet

*Preferably catch a water taxi from Soufrière or take the rough track at the north end of Soufrière beach, about 1 mile. The first part is very steep and rough and taxis often refuse to go up it. Map 1, H2, p205 See also p104*

This is an absolute must if you enjoy snorkelling. The area in front of the Anse Chastanet Hotel is a buoyed off **marine reserve**, stretching from the west point at Grand Caille North to Chamin Cove. Only the hotel boats and local fishermen's canoes are allowed in. The south end near the jetty is superb but keep within the roped off area; the north end is also good with some rocks to explore, but avoid the middle where boats come in. The hotel has a good and inexpensive restaurant (although if you are on a budget you may prefer to take a picnic) and the dive shop is extremely helpful, they will hire out equipment by the hour, see p157 for information on diving. The *Unicorn* and other day sail boats stop here for snorkelling and a swim in the afternoon on their return to Castries. The beach, like nearly all others in St Lucia, is public.

## Eastern Caribbean Butterfly House

Lovers Lane, Soufrière **T** 4597429, stluciabutterflyhouse@ yahoo.com *Daily 1000-1700. US$6/EC$16. 4 blocks from RC church, just off Sir Arthur Lewis St. Map 1, I2, p205 See also Kids p169*

The Butterfly House is the only one in the Windwards. Imported pupae from Central America and the Caribbean are hatched and grown in a small house then set loose. Over 60 varieties are flying around freely in the tropical garden setting.

## Diamond Gardens and Baths

SoufrièreT 4524759/4597565, soufestate@candw.lc *Mon-Sat 1000-1700, Sun and holidays 1000-1500. EC$7, children EC$3, EC$7 to use the outdoor hot baths, EC$10 for private bath. Only official guides are allowed in, do not accept offers from those at the gates. All the car parks are free, no matter what some people may tell you. From the square take Sir Arthur Lewis Street east past the church and look for a right hand turning to reach the Diamond Gardens. Map 1, I2, p205*

These lovely botanical gardens and mineral baths can be difficult to locate (or expensive if forced to ask) as there are no road signs in Soufrière so follow the directions above. The **baths** were developed in 1784 after Baron de Laborie sent samples taken from sulphur springs near the Diamond River to Paris for analysis. They found minerals present which were equivalent to those found in the spa town of Aix-la-Chapelle and were said to be effective against rheumatism and other complaints. The French King ordered baths to be built. Despite being destroyed by Brigands in 1836, they were eventually rebuilt in 1925 by André duBoulay and can be used by the public. The estate owner, Mrs Joan Devaux, André duBoulay's daughter, plans to carry out an archaeological restoration of the baths as they existed in the 18th century and the original plans have been found in archives in Paris. The **gardens** are better than ever; well maintained and many native plants can be seen. A nature trail follows a ridge through a forest of red cedar and mahogany, ending at the estate's restored sugar mill and waterwheel, which still turns.

● *The Soufrière Estate used to produce lime oil which was stored in vats and taken on board ships travelling between the West Indies and British ports. British sailors drank a spoonful of the vitamin C-rich oil every day to combat scurvy and for that reason became known as 'Limeys'.*

## Toraille waterfall

On road to Fond St Jacques. *Daily 0900-1700. EC$5/US$2.*
*Map 1, 1 I2, p205*

A path leads through lovely gardens stocked with anthuriums and
ginger lilies to a single 18-m high waterfall into a pool 1-m deep.
The water is refreshingly cool and if you stand under the fall the
force is quite painful although apparently you will feel ten years
younger if you manage to get under it. The waterfall is close to the
road and included in many tours to the Sulphur Springs. These
come mostly in the morning from Castries or Rodney Bay, so if you
go early or late you should have the place to yourself.

## Stonefield Estate

Just south of Soufrière,  on the way to the Sulphur Springs
**T** 4530777, www.stonefieldvillas.com  *Ask at reception for
permission to visit and directions to the trail.  Map 1, I2, p205*

Stonefield Estate, on the way to the Sulphur Springs, has very fine
petroglyphs, which are used on the company logo. They are
believed to date from AD 350 and can be found along the estate's
nature trail through the forest. This used to be a cocoa plantation,
but now the family concentrates on providing luxurious villa
accommodation, a spectacular view of the Pitons and a restaurant,
the *Mango Tree*, see p123.

## Sulphur Springs

On the Vieux Fort road out of Soufrière. *Daily 0900-1700. EC$3.
Compulsory tour with guide takes about 30 mins. Take the Vieux Fort
road between wooden houses halfway along south side of Soufrière
square. Follow the road for about 2 miles and you will see a sign on
the left and smell the springs. Gift shop is more expensive than
Castries market.  Map 1, I3, p205  See also Kids p169*

Originally a huge volcano about 3 miles in diameter, it collapsed some 40,000 years ago leaving the west part of the rim empty (where you drive in). The sign welcomes you to the world's only drive-in volcano, although actually you have to stop at a car park. The sulphur spring is the only one still active, although there are seven cones within the old crater as well as the pitons which are thought to be volcanic plugs. There has been much geothermal research here since 1974. The Island Arawaks believed their god *Yokahu* slept in the volcano and it was therefore the site of human sacrifices. The Caribs were less superstitious but still named it *Qualibou*, the place of death. There is a small village of about 40 inhabitants located inside the rim of the volcano. A good path leads up steps to the stream where you can bathe but it is not very appealing and the guides don't give you much time to stop and think about it. Here the water is at 25°C, but in the concrete pool alongside, built years ago for health purposes, the temperature reaches 45°C. Further up, from the main viewing platform, you can see over a moonscape of bubbling, mineral rich, grey mud pools. One of these pools, known as 'Gabriel's hole', was created when a guide jumped around too much. He received second-degree burns from the waist down, but survived after medical attention in Martinique and now works as a fisherman. The hole is still growing and no one is now allowed near the pools, with visitors confined to the viewing platform. The mud reaches a temperature of 100°C although the main vent gets up to 171°C. The water comes from the sea via vents as well as from an underground lake, and at full moon when there is a high tide you can see geysers spouting up to 7 m high.

## Petit Piton
*Map 1, I2 205*

Petit Piton is 743 m (2437 ft) high, a volcanic plug rising sheer out of the sea and since June 2004 a UNESCO World Heritage Site, along with its sister, Gros Piton see p84. It is a focal point of all views around Soufrière and because it is closer to the town, people often think it is higher than Gros Piton. It is possible to climb Petit Piton, an extremely steep ascent, but it is not encouraged. It used to be restricted but the ruling appears to have lapsed. Local guides will take you up for about US$50, but it is dangerous and by doing it you are damaging the ecology of the mountain. Better just to look and not touch.

## Jalousie

*Take the turning opposite the Morne Coubaril Estate (closed 2004) on the unsigned concrete road.*   Map 1, I2, p205

In the valley between Petit Piton and Gros Piton, a luxury all-inclusive resort, Jalousie Plantation (formerly Hilton) Resort and Spa, has been built despite complaints from ecological groups and evidence from archaeologists that it is located on a major Amerindian site. An important burial ground is believed to be under the tennis courts and there have been many finds of petroglyphs and pottery. A rather fine **petroglyph** is at the back of the beach in front of Lord Glenconner's Bang Between the Pitons. Lord Glenconner used to own much of the land here. Halfway along the drive to Jalousie you will see a little sign to a small, warm waterfall on your left. Someone will collect about US$2 for access. Relax in the warm waters.

## Fond Doux Estate

3 miles from Soufrière **T**   *Daily 0800-1600. EC$15. See Heritage Tours, p30.*   Map 1, J2, p205

The Fond Doux Estate was one of the first established by the French in the 18th century and covers 135 acres up in the hills. It has been in continuous production for over 250 years, growing first cocoa and coffee, then sugar, and is still producing cocoa, using

## Liberté, Fraternité, Egalité

After the French Revolution, activists entered St Lucia around the time that Haiti was undergoing its black Revolution and fomented civil unrest between slaves and planters. France abolished slavery in 1794, but a request for liberty by slaves on St Lucia was met by brutal repression by the local militia. The delay in implementing the emancipation was due to a British invasion about the time of the declaration. France and Britain were at war from 1793 and their colonies were part of the battlefield. A British expedition arrived in 1794 but were met by a revolt of white planters and free blacks. They formed the local Revolutionary Party and took to the hills, becoming known as *L'Armée Française dans les bois*, or Brigands, with a stronghold in Soufrière. Guerrilla warfare brought the destruction of plantations all over the island and many bloody battles.

In 1795 the British forces left their garrison in Castries to attack the revolutionaries at Soufrière. A French expedition from Guadeloupe came with reinforcements, a total of 600 troops and some cannon, to join the local fighting force of 250 St Lucians and 300 maroons, or escaped slaves, around the Fond Doux estate. The British marched overland from Vieux Fort and reached Fond Doux on April 22, a week after leaving Castries, but they were ambushed in a heavy cross fire of cannon and musketry. After a day of fierce fighting the British retreated to Castries. They later suffered further defeats at Gros Islet and Vigie and on 19 June they fled, leaving the revolutionaries in control of the island. The slaves were freed, but a year later the British returned under the command of Generals Moore and Abercromby and in 1798 ended the Brigand wars and brought back slavery.

traditional processing methods. The Fond Doux plantation house built in 1864 is a typical single storey wooden construction with a veranda and outside kitchen, surrounded by pleasant gardens adapted from a cocoa plantation where you can see nutmeg growing, grapefruit trees, cinnamon, coffee and lots of flowers. Surplus herbs, spices and food crops are sold in the owners' supermarket in town. The owners still live in the house but doors and windows are left open for visitors to look in. The estate is primarily open for tour groups who receive a tour showing traditional methods of grinding cocoa and how cocoa grows, identifying flowers and fruit trees, as well as a buffet lunch of local dishes. You can also walk up the hill to a Brigands' hideout, an escape trail which takes you up a steep slope to the Chateaubelair ridge, from where you can see the Pitons and the sea, a great view from a different angle. There are also some military ruins on the estate along the East Ruins Trail. A major battle took place here in 1795 between the French Republican Revolutionaries and the British and it is assumed that the buildings were constructed by French engineers before then.

### Gros Piton

Gros Piton Tour Guide Association, **T** 4599748, assisted by the Forestry Department, **T**4502231 Ext 316, Fond Gens Libre Tour Guides Association, **T**4593833. *Daily 0900-1500. A guide costs about EC$20, but if you have your own transport you can do it on your own. Map 1, K3, p205*

Gros Piton, part of the UNESCO World Heritage site, is squat and fat compared with Petit Piton, but is in fact higher, at 770 m (2526 ft). Studies have been done on the fauna and flora of the mountain, which show that there are four life zones, depending on the amount of moisture received: a dry, middle, mountain, and upper mountain climate belt, which include cloud forest, rain forest and elfin woodland. At the base of the mountain there is some agriculture including goats grazing, charcoal making and some vegetable plots, but otherwise it is free of human disturbance because of the inhospitable terrain. Some 148 plant species have been found on Gros Piton, together with 27 species of birds. Four species endemic to the island live here: the St Lucia oriole, St Lucia black finch, St Lucia warbler and the St Lucia wren.

South of Soufrière, near Union Vale estate, is the Gros Piton trail. The village of Fond Gens Libre, the first settlement by freed slaves, is at the base of the mountain, accessible by jeep or high-clearance car although you will have to ford a couple of streams. The hike up and back is about four hours through the different ecosystems with stops to look at Brigand caves and tunnels. It is strenuous, so you must be in good physical condition. It should not be attempted in wet weather. There are also more cultural and less strenuous walks in the area, visiting historical sites and local artisans making coal pots, baskets or floor mats. Contact Jimmy Haynes, **T** 4599748, grospitontours@candw.lc.

### Enbas Saut Trail

6 miles east of Soufrière via Fond St Jacques. Forestry Department, **T** 4502231 Ext 316, forestrails@slumaffe.org   *Trail open daily 0830-1500. US$10 with or without guide. the road is poor, high clearance essential.*   *Map 1, I4, p205*

This trail in the 19,000-acre Central Rainforest Reserve is in dense rainforest, with a good chance of seeing a variety of woodland birds. You will hear the St Lucia parrot even if you are not lucky enough to see it. The vegetation is a mix of rainforest, cloud forest and elfin woodland, with glorious views of the three peaks of Piton Canarie, Piton Troumassée and Morne Gimie. The 2½-mile trail has been cut down to the Troumassée river, where there are a couple of waterfalls and a pool where you can bathe. It is a moderate to strenuous hike as there are 2,112 steps down and back up again and the hillside is steep, not recommended for those with breathing difficulties or heart problems. You can also expect to get wet and muddy and good footwear is essential. There are a couple of river crossings to negotiate. At the falls there are picnic tables and a screen behind which you can change your clothes for swimming. There are toilets at the Rangers' station at the start of the trail.

## Edmond Rainforest Trail

*Forestry Department, T 4502231 Ext 316, forestrails@slumaffe.org Mon-Fri 0830-1500. US$10. Weekends by arrangement at extra cost. Reached on same poor road as Enbas Saut Trail. Map 1, J2, p205*

This hike is easy to moderate on a trail through the heart of the island in the forest reserve. There are glimpses of the Caribbean Sea and a magnificent view of Morne Gimie, the island's highest peak. The Forestry guide will point out bromeliads, orchids, strangler figs and other forest plants as well as the many forest birds. With prior arrangement you can hike all the way across the island, joining up with the Des Cartiers Rainforest Trail in the east, see p63. These hiking tours cost US$25.

## Choiseul

*Map 1, K3, p205*

The road from Soufrière to Vieux Fort takes about 40 minutes by car. The branch of the road through Fond St Jacques (with another church painted by Dunstan St Omer) runs through lush rainforest. In a few miles the road rapidly descends from Victoria Junction at 366 m (1,200 ft) to the coastal plain at Choiseul. **Choiseul** is a quaint old West Indian village: there is a fish market and church on the beach, where you can swim. **Caraibe Point** is the last place on St Lucia where Caribs still survive, a small community of potters living in simple thatched houses. North of Choiseul is a **petroglyph**, visible from the road, but you must park and then

walk a little way. Outlined in white, under a protective roof, it is just down the cliff toward the sea. On the south side of Choiseul, the **Art and Craft Development Centre** teaches skills in bamboo handicrafts. You can buy pottery, baskets and carvings and there
is an excellent selection, worth a visit (*open Mon-Fri 0900-1600, T 4593226*).

---

## Balenbouche
Southeast of Choiseul, www.balenbouche.com   *Map 1, L3, p205*

Balenbouche Estate is an old sugar plantation on 150 acres where you can stay in the lovely old estate home or in a cottage; good local food. There is usually an event in the annual Jazz Festival held here. There is also an ancient aqueduct connected in some way to the irrigation system at Balenbouche and the canal that carried water to the wheel at the sugar mill. The path from the house to the ruins of the sugar mill is easy and very picturesque. From the mill another path follows the route down which the barrels used to be rolled to the shore. There are rock basins here. The Estate is still a working farm, growing fruit and veg for the local markets and the grounds are stocked with mature mango, breadfruit and flamboyant trees, amongst others.

There are Arawak petroglyphs on rocks in the Balenbouche River. If you wade along the river and look up, you will see faces staring down at you from the top of the ravine, the work of the Amerindians who used to live on the terraces above the deep ravine. Evidence of their farming tools have been found there, including red flakes of jasper (red flint) and stone artifacts such as axes, adzes and hammers, used instead of metal tools. You will probably need somebody to show you the way from Balenbouche Estate or Saltibus. A team from the University of Bristol did an archaeological dig here in 2001 and an exploratory trip along the River Dorée, where there are a number of other petroglyphs.

In the mist of the sea there is a horned island with deep green harbours...
...a place of light with luminous valleys under thunderous clouds...
...a volcano, stinking with Sulphur, has made it a healing place.

*Omeros by Derek Walcott*

Sleeping

St Lucia has a wide and varied selection of hotels, guesthouses, apartments and villas. The majority of hotels are small, friendly and offer flexible service. They cater for all budgets, from the height of luxury at Ladera Resort or Anse Chastanet, to simple guest houses in Gros Islet where you fall into bed after the Friday night jump-up. Most of the larger hotels (the *Club St Lucia*, the three *Sandals* resorts and *Rex* hotels, the *Windjammer Landing* and the *St James Club*) are all-inclusive. Rodney Bay is the place to stay if you want the beach, restaurants and nightlife on your doorstep, while the marina makes excursions convenient by boat, whether for day sails, diving or whale watching. The northwest has the best beaches of golden sand and hotels here are convenient for golf and cricket, but still within striking distance of the action. Several hotels around Soufrière enjoy fabulous views of the Pitons and the coast, perched on hillsides in beautiful tropical gardens and forests; truly peaceful, but you will have to arrange car hire or taxis to get around or go to restaurants.

**Sleeping codes**

Elsewhere, many of the hotels are remote resorts, providing everything their guests need for a relaxing holiday or honeymoon in romantic locations. Castries is obviously good for business travellers, but there is a beach and it is convenient for people who want to explore the island by bus. A good-value guest house will probably include breakfast, which may be anything from a slice of fruit and a bread roll to a full cooked spread of eggs and bacon or saltfish, allowing you to snack at lunchtime and afford a slap up dinner in the evening.

▸▸ *See also Camping p107 and Villa rental p107*

# Castries

**AL-B Auberge Seraphine**, Vigie Marina, **T** 4532073, www.aubergeseraphine.com *Map 2, D1, p206* A gleaming white, modern hotel on the edge of the harbour close to Vigie airport with 22 rooms on two levels with a/c and TV, a terrace and pool with good views of the boats, and a restaurant. It is attractive and well-run and even flocks of egrets fly in to roost here.

**A Cara Suites**, La Pansée, overlooking Castries, **T** 458 CARA, www.carahotels.com *Only a 10-min walk down the hill to the centre but a strenuous 15 mins back up. Map 1, C4, p204* The reception, restaurant – with a fabulous view over Castries and the harbour – and business facilities are divided by the pool from the large modern block of 54 comfortable rooms, with a/c, TV, VCR, video library, minibar, but worth it for the magnificent view and excellent value for business or pleasure. The restaurant is reasonable and there is a buffet breakfast and lunch; vegetarians may however find their options are limited.

**B-C  t'bell Maison**, Vide Bouteille, **T** 4508246, tbel@candw.lc *Map 1, C4, p204*  Run by the helpful Basil Belizaire and his niece Florencia, the rooms are clean and white and have fan or a/c and are quiet even though the main road to Gros Islet is 100 m below.

**C  Chesterfield**, southern end of Bridge St, **T/F** 4521295, *Map 2, H2, p206*. Central, with 14 a/c rooms and a tropical garden; some rooms have a balcony and a great view over Castries. There is use of the kitchen and it is excellent value.

**C  Harbour Light Inn**, City Gate, **T** 4523506, **F** 4519455, *Map 1, C4, p204*  Just a three-minute walk to Vigie Beach, at the end of Vigie airport runway, with parking, 16 rooms, a/c or fan, with private bathrooms, cable TV, and a balcony all round the building giving a panorama of the west coast and airplanes. Restaurant and bar.

**E  Chateau Blanc**, on Morne Doudon Rd, **T** 4521851, **F** 4527967, *Map 2, G6, p206*  Predictably painted white, this is a two-storey house with seven rooms, all with fan and bathroom. It is basic but in a good central location on a hill, within walking distance of the centre. Food available on request.

**E  Thelma's Guesthouse**, Waterworks Rd, **T** 4527313, *Map 2, H6, p206*  No sign; look for the white building with green awnings. Rooms have a shared bathroom and lounge and use of the kitchen. A central location and owner Theresa Debique is warm and caring.

## Morne Fortune

**AL-A  Top of the Morne Apartments, T** 4523603, **F** 4523603, www.topothemorne.com *Map 1, D4, p204*  Twelve apartments or studios with one or two bedrooms sleeping one to five people, all with verandas giving a spectacular view over Castries and the coast and a pool; very friendly. Car rental can be arranged at good rates. Rum shop, bakery and grocery nearby, good restaurants within walking distance.

**C  Bon Appetit**, Top of the Morne, **T** 4522757, **F** 4527967.  *Map 1, D4, p204*  Beautiful view over Castries and the coast from the restaurant and guest house, which is clean and friendly. There are three rooms with private bathroom, cable TV, breakfast included. Book early for an evening meal in the popular restaurant, see p114.

**E  Morne Fortune Guest House**, Top of the Morne, **T** 4521742, *Across the road from the Sir Arthur Lewis Community College campus.  Map 1, D4 p204*  This spotless guesthouse has single rooms big enough for two, shared bathrooms, spacious, well-equipped kitchen for self-catering, and is run by Mrs Regina Willie who is helpful and informative. Restaurants  and a bakery are close by. Monthly rates available. Good access to public transport.

## Coubaril

**B-C** (per person)  **The Nunnery**, **T** 4521282, *Head south to the Morne junction at the Shell station, then right turn down hill, take second right.  Map 1, I2, p205*  The Benedictine nuns have 22 rooms with private bathrooms, a/c, fans, MAP, in a lovely, secluded and tranquil wooded setting – a 15-minute easy walk along a wooded road to frequent public transport. The chapel is packed for Christmas Eve mass.

# North to Rodney Bay and Gros Islet

## Gablewoods Mall

**B** **Friendship Inn**, Sunny Acres, **T** 4524201, **F** 4532635, *Opposite side of road from Sandals near the Mall. Map 1, C4, p204* Convenient if you come in to Vigie airport after dark and want somewhere close by,10 one-bedroom apartments with a kitchenette overlook the main road and have a restaurant offering local dishes for breakfast and dinner at moderate prices. There is a daily happy hour and barbecue specials beside the small pool on Saturday nights and baby-sitting services are available.

**D-E** **The Golden Arrow**, on highway to Gros Islet, **T** 4501832, **F** 4502329, *Map 1, C4, p204* This modern house has 15 pleasant rooms, with private bathrooms, a friendly host and a balcony and veranda from which you can see down to the bay. It is within walking distance of beach and bus. Breakfast and dinner available.

**D** **Parrots Hideaway**, nr Gablewoods Mall, **T/F** 4520726, *Map1, C4, p204* Your charming hostess has four rooms each with private bathroom, and five rooms sharing two bathrooms. Discounts are given for longer stays. There is a bar, and restaurant offering a Creole menu.

## Choc Bay

**L-AL** **Villa Beach Cottages**, Choc Beach, **T** 4502884, www.villabeachcottages.com *Map1, B4, p204* These beachfront cottages with gingerbread fretwork, wooden shutters and jalousies are sandwiched between the main road and the sea next to *The Wharf* restaurant and have either one or two bedrooms with four-poster beds, a/c, fans, TV, phone, data ports, kitchen, living room, and a balcony with hammocks. Derek Walcott spent his holidays in what is now called the 'Nobel Cottage', a lovely honeymoon villa, and there are nine new villa suites, *Coconuts* restaurant with bar and grill, car rental, tours desk. Alternatively, or in combination, under same ownership is *La Dauphine Estate* (see p105).

## Labrellotte Bay

**LL-L  Windjammer Landing**, **T** 4520913, www.wlv-resort.com
*Map 1, B4, p204*  A beautiful luxury resort in a lovely hillside setting, but isolated – it's a 30-minute walk to a bus route or EC\$20 taxi to Rodney Bay: one-bedroomed suites clustered together, two- to four-bedroomed villas spread out with their own plunge pool, white and multilevel in the style of a southern Spanish development. Activities include tennis and watersports, on a much-improved beach. Good international food aimed at pleasing everybody. Honeymoon, family and diving packages.

## Rodney Bay

**LL-L  Rex St Lucian**, Reduit Beach, **T** 4528351, rexstlucian@candw.lc  *Map 3, E5, p207*  Right on the beach, 120 all-inclusive a/c rooms with restaurants, pools, entertainment, good sports facilities, and a convenient location. On either side are two other Rex properties, the sister hotels: **Papillon** all-inclusive to the south and the 98-suite **Royal St Lucian**, (which isn't all-inclusive) to the north with swim-up bar and health spa. Facilities for wheelchair users.

**LL-AL  Marlin Quay**, Gros Islet, **T** 4520393, www.marlin-quay.com
*Map 3, F6, p207*  On the waterfront in Rodney Bay, a Mediterranean-style villa resort offering a variety of very comfortable rooms and spacious well equipped studios, one- and two-bedroom apartments, and two- and three-bedroom terraced villas, with views over the

lagoon, some with roof-top Jacuzzis and sun-decks, and verandas. There are restaurants and two pools, one small and one 40 ft long. Highly recommended for families or couples.

**L-AL  The Village Inn and Spa at Rodney Bay**, T 4583300, villageinn@candw.lc *Formerly the Rainbow, further down the same road as Rex and Royal. Map 3, E6, p207* Across the road from the beach, this colourful pleasant hotel has 76 a/c rooms, tennis, a fitness centre, pool, beach towels, snack bar, internet access, and is linked with the Cap Estate Golf Course and golf packages are offered. Breakfast is included.

**L-AL  Tuxedo Villas**, T 4528553, www.nbi.net/tuxedo *Next to the Ginger Lily Hotel opposite the entrance to Spinnakers. Map 3, E6, p207* One minute from Reduit Beach, this stylish pink modern building is built around a pool and offers four one-bedroom and six two-bedroom self-catering apartments with a/c, TV, phone, maid service, kitchenette.

**L-A  Ginger Lily**, T 4580300, www.thegingerlilyhotel.com *Right opposite Spinnakers, Map 3, E6, p207* Eleven apartments ranging from superior deluxe (the cheapest) to executive (the most expensive), each of which have a fridge, TV, phone and fan are conveniently located opposite the Yacht Club and the beach. Very colourful on the outside with yellow walls, red roof and blue umbrellas around the pool, which has a picture of a ginger lily on the bottom, but inside the rooms are restrained, with white walls and muted colours in the furnishings.

**AL  Caribbean Jewel**, T 4529199, www.caribbeanjewel resort.com *Map 3, F4, p207* On the hillside at the south end of the bay with a glorious view over to Pigeon Island and to Martinique on a clear day. Rooms and suites are a good size and all have a/c and TV and some have kitchens and Jacuzzis. Executive suites have two bedrooms, living/dining room and two bathrooms. There are several pools at different levels, including a children's pool. It is a hike down to the beach through the bush, or you can go round by the road to the Rex. Restaurant on site, *The Villa*, see p118.

**AL  Harmony Marina Suites**, **T** 4528756, **F** 4528677, *On lagoon, close to beach  Map 3, F6, p207*  These locally owned studios and apartments are comfortable and convenient and have a restaurant, bar, pool, and mini-mart on site. Watersports including canoeing.

**AL-A  Bay Gardens Inn**, **T** 4528200, www.baygardensinn.com *Right next door to JQ's Mall  Map 3, F6, p207*  This is a well-managed, medium-sized modern hotel with 32 a/c rooms, TV, pool, bar, restaurant and conference facilities. It is an extension of Bay Gardens Hotel and both host conferences and workshops so are fairly lively. The main Castries road is outside with frequent buses. Berthia Parle, the general manager, is the head of the St Lucia Hotel and Tourism Association and was elected the first female President of the Caribbean Hotel Association for 2004.

**AL-A  Coco Kreole**, **T** 4520712, www.cocokreole.com  *Map 3, F5, p207*  A small hotel in a convenient location close to restaurants. The rooms are designed in pairs so that they can connect to make a family suite and, although not large, are adequately equipped with TV, a/c, fridge, coffee maker, good lighting and king size beds but there is only limited wardrobe space and no chair. The bar overlooks a small pool in the rear garden and a buffet breakfast, included in the room rate, is served here.

**AL-A  MJI**, **T** 4528090, www.mjivilla.com  *Just off the main road opposite Bay Gardens Inn  Map 3, F6, p207*  This small plantation-house style modern hotel, very elegant with white walls and verandas and red roof has19 rooms, studios and two-bedroom apartment, all with a/c, TV. Rates are negotiable according to season. The pool to the front of the villa has a view over Rodney Bay and there is a spa on site for massages and facials.

**A-B  Mango Sands**, T 4529800, www.razmatazstlucia.com *Map 3, E5, p207* Two attractive twin-bedded rooms behind *Razmataz* restaurant, see p118, each with veranda, fridge, tea- and coffee-making facilities and a short walk to the beach across the road. The rate includes fruit and pastries for breakfast, tax and service. No smoking.

**B-D  Villa Zandoli**, T 4528898, www.saintelucie.com *Just down the road from Rumours restaurant. Map 3, E6, p207* This small, cheap, six-bedroom guest house has fairly basic rooms (doubles, twins and single) with mosquito nets, cable TV, and a/c at extra cost. Excursions and activities can be arranged. The family speaks English, French, Spanish and Kwéyòl. The kitchen is available if you want to cook, and there is also a living room with TV, CD player and books. Continental breakfast is included; internet access, laundry services, airport transfers are offered.

## Gros Islet

**L-C  Tropical Breeze**, 38 Massie St, Massade, Gros Islet, T/F 4500589, www.stluonestop/tropical *Map 1, A5, p204* The modern white guest house with bedrooms and one- to four-bedroom apartments, fully equipped with TV, phone and kitchen overlooks Rodney Bay. Bed and Breakfast is available, or meal plans with good home Creole cooking. The building backs on to the police station and is within easy reach of the cricket ground or the venues for the Jazz Festival. Excellent value for groups.

**B  Glencastle Resort**, Massade, on hillside overlooking Rodney Bay, T 4500833, www.glencastleresort.net *On hillside overlooking Rodney Bay. Map 1, A5, p204* This new luxurious resort aims for

French colonial style with pink walls and white balconies, and has 17 a/c rooms, pool and restaurant and is good value for money.

**B-D B&B/Anette's Hotel**, on Gros Islet highway, Massade, **T** 4508689, **F** 4508134. *Map 1, A5, p204* This B&B is within walking distance of the Marina, beaches and Pigeon Island causeway. It has a/c, fans, kitchenettes in some rooms but it is noisy at night with loud music, especially country and western.

**B-D My Helen's Inn**, **T** 4508301, *Down a side road leading to the fisheries complex and the marina, right by the boats opposite Eagle's Inn on the other side of the water. Map 3, D6, p207* The rooms in this 14-room guest house are clean and well-furnished but nothing fancy with fans or a/c and TV in some. All have a view of the sea or the marina from the balconies and kitchen facilities are available. They can take groups of up to 26 for reunions or school parties.

**C La Panache**, Cas-en-Bas Rd, **T** 4500765, augustinh@candw.lc *Map 1, A5, p204* Run by the helpful and friendly Henry Augustin and also Roger Graveson, who is working with the Forestry Department to complete a listing of the plants of St Lucia and can give information on Atlantic beaches, coastal walking and birdwatching tours. Four clean two-bedroom apartments, all with balcony, bathroom, fridge, cooking facilities, hot water, insect screens and fans, gardens with plants labelled, good meals, snacks during day, see p119

**C-E Alexander's Guesthouse**, Mary Thérèse St, **T** 4508610, **F** 4508014, *Map 3, D6, p207* A new building one minute from the beach this is clean and safe with use of a kitchen. Friendly and helpful host and credit cards are accepted.

**D Bay Mini Guest House**, Bay St, **T** 4508956, *Map 3, D5, p207* The rooms here are spacious with fan and bathroom and there are two studios with kitchenettes, painted bright orange, in this guest house on the beach run by Klaus Kretz who speaks German and English. Minimum stay two nights.

**D Nelson's Furnished Apartments**, Cas-en-Bas Rd, **T** 4508275, *300 m uphill from main road to Castries. Map 1, A5, p204* Run by Marilyn and Davy, the apartments have hot water, fan, TV, mosquito net and balcony with view over Rodney Bay; towels and toilet paper are supplied and there is free but slow internet access.

**D The Wall/Paradise Beach Hotel**, 1A St George St, **T** 4500388. *Behind the restaurant, see p119 Map 3, D5, p207* Right on the beach and run by the very hospitable Cletus Hippolyte, the rooms here are clean with fan and shower.

## The north and northeast coasts

**LL CAPri**, Smugglers Cove, **T** 4500009, www.capristlucia.com *Map 3, B6, p207* A modern villa with sea view which used to be the Chinese embassy, now British-run, in a peaceful location. The 10 a/c rooms have, four-poster beds with mosquito nets, white walls and white tiled floors, fans and TV. There is an open-air bar and wooden deck by the small pool. It is walking distance to Smugglers Beach (used by *Club St Lucia*) and guests can use the facilities of *Le Sport*, an all-inclusive hotel in the area.

## East coast to Vieux Fort

### East coast

**B Manje Domi**, Desruisseaux, **T** 4550729, manje-domi@candw.lc *5 km south of Micoud, turn at Anse Ger junction, 1½ km to guesthouse on top of hill Map 1, J6, p205* This pleasant low-key guesthouse, with restaurant and bar, has four small but immaculate rooms, each with patio, screens, fan or a/c, TV, in a countryside setting with full breakfast included. Meals are seafood and fresh local vegetables and fruits. The name means 'eat, sleep' in Kwéyòl.

**B-C Foxgrove Inn**, Mon Repos, **T** 4553271, www.foxgroveinn.com *Map 1, H6, p205* On a hillside with a wonderful view of Praslin Bay and Fregate Islands, this Swiss/St Lucian owned hotel is just by Mamiku Gardens and a good base for exploring the east coast. It is not fancy but has 12 comfortable bedrooms with small shower and TV, fan, and balcony (ask for a view to the front), a two-bedroom apartment. a large pool, nature trails, riding stables and good food. Breakfast is included and meal plans are available. Discounts for long stay. German and French spoken.

## Vieux Fort

**AL-B Juliette's Lodge**, Beanfield, Vieux Fort, **T** 4545300, www.julietteslodge.com *Down a road opposite the entrance to the airport. Map 1, L6, p205* The best option for accommodation in this area, with good value rooms and apartments of varying sizes, with balconies, a/c, TV, some with fridge, all with ocean view, small bathrooms, small pool, restaurant with view of runway framed by Maria Islands and the lighthouse, bar, 10 minutes to beach, run by Juliette and Andrew Paul who are hospitable and helpful.

**C-D City View Guesthouse**, New Dock Lane, **T** 4548133, cityview@stluciaweb.com *Map 1, L6, p205* Near the centre of Vieux Fort but within easy reach of the beach and local attractions, these self-contained cottages, with a/c, TV, VCR, stove and fridge, are simple but cheap.

**D-F St Martin**, on main street, **T/F** 4546674, *Map 1, L6, p205* Clean, friendly, cooking and washing facilities.

## Marigot Bay

**LL-A Marigot Beach Club**, on the north shore of the bay, **T** 4514974, www.marigotdiveresort.com  *Map 1, E3, p204* Waterfront restaurant and bar, *Café Paradis* open from 0800, *Doolittle's* restaurant for lunch and dinner with live entertainment most nights. Lots of activities including sailing, kayaking, *Dive Fair Helen* PADI dive shop, pool, sundeck, beach. Accommodation ranges from studios with kitchenette, fans, bathroom and patio to very pretty, light and airy villas with one to three bedrooms on hillside. Mobile phones in every room.

**AL The Inn On the Bay**, **T** 4514260, www.saint-lucia.com *Along a ½ mile of unpaved road  Map 1, E3, p204* Only five spacious rooms in a white West-Indian style building with wrap around balconies up on the hill overlooking Marigot Bay with a great view from the pool, continental breakfast included, tours and car hire arranged and complimentary transport down to the bay. Run by friendly Normand Viau and Louise Boucher.

**AL-C Cliff House**, **T** 4527921, www.cliff-house.com  *Next door to The Inn On The Bay and just before you fall off the cliff.  Map 1, E3, p204* Away from Marigot Bay activities, secluded with beautiful views, this rental home with its red roof is a landmark for sailors coming into harbour. Previously owned by the Boudreau family, who owned most of Marigot Bay in the 1960s, it is now in the possession of Alice Bagshaw of silk screen factory. Two bedrooms with four-poster beds and en-suite bathrooms, breakfast included, spectacular view, kitchen and dining area adjacent to the sitting room, all with Spanish clay tiled floors, wrap-around veranda for panoramic views from your hammock, car hire and airport transfers arranged, daily maid service. Away from Marigot Bay activities, secluded with beautiful views.

**A Villa de la Gratia T** 4583119, www.villadelagratia.com  *Map 1, E3, p204*  Twelve rooms, with a/c, fans, fridge, TV and email, overlook the harbour with a pool and pool bar, convenient for sailing and just two minutes' walk to the beach. Breakfast is included. Next door is *JJ's* restaurant, see p122, which gets bigger all the time and specializes in seafood and loud music.

## Anse La Raye

**LL-L Ti Kaye Village**, just south of Anse La Raye, **T** 4568101, tikaye@candw.lc  *Map 1, F2, p204*  An unbelievably romantic spot and popular for weddings and honeymoons: white wooden cottages with decorative fretwork, large verandas with rocking chairs and double hammocks – all with sea views, although some are a little obscured by trees. The large bedrooms with louvred windows, but also a/c and fans, are prettily decorated with liberal use of bougainvillea on four-poster beds and towels. Some rooms have their own plunge pool and there are outside showers. The main pool is by the bar and restaurant which serve good food and an extensive cocktail list (try the *Piton Snow*: white rum, triple sec, coconut cream, frozen). A mere 169 steps will take you down the cliff to Anse Cochon beach, one of the prettiest.

## Soufrière and around

**LL Ladera Resort**, **T** 4597323, www.ladera-stlucia.com  *Map 1, I2, p205*  Every possible luxury is here in an intimate and spectacular setting between Gros Piton and Petit Piton. Each of the 24 rooms, 1,000 ft up, lacks a west wall over a drop that only Superman could climb, providing an uninterrupted view of the Pitons. There are one- to three-bedroom villas and suites, very cold plunge pools, 60s-style swimming pools, used to film *Superman II*, a lovely restaurant, lots of birds – and mosquitoes.

**LL-L Anse Chastanet**, **T** 4597000, www.ansechastanet.com
*Map 1, H1-2, p205* These luxurious and airy, hillside and beachside suites, constructed in different styles from wooden lodge to white Spanish, are all really special and have open balconies and stunning views in every direction. The only drawback is the walk uphill after overindulging at dinner. Here you will find the best scuba diving on the island, with a consistently highly rated dive operation and diving packages available, as well as other watersports, tennis, a spa, a lovely beach setting, restaurants on the beach and halfway up the hill, live music in the evenings and walks and excursions. The existing suites are practically invisible from the sea, although in 2004 a block of more rooms were being built up the hillside.

**LL-L Mago Estate Hotel**, **T** 4595880, www.mago-hotel.com
*Map 1, H2, p205* Originally a private home, built by an architect into the cliff and incorporating all the natural and geological features, now a small, luxury hotel with 10 beautiful rooms and suites framed by bougainvillea overlooking the bay, Pitons and mountains, with four-poster beds, huge louvred windows folding out to uninterrupted views, and open bathrooms. Spacious suites have plunge pools, breakfast is included, MAP available. The pool bar is in the roots of a huge mango tree, with a tree house above, the lounge bar built into the rock formation and mango trees, and there is a Yin & Yang health farm if you need a detox.

**LL-L Stonefield Estate**, **T** 4597037, www.stonefieldvillas.com
*Map 1, I2, p205* Owned and managed by the Brown family, this small hillside villa resort is incredibly romantic, with stunning views of Petit Piton and overlooking Malgrétoute beach. Villas sleep two to eight with outdoor showers, kitchens, hammocks on the

veranda and many have plunge pools. A 26-acre former cocoa estate, the grounds are forested, with many fruit trees and birds and a nature trail to some petroglyphs, which are the resort's logo. There is a good restaurant by the main swimming pool, but a shuttle will take you to Soufrière if you want to shop for food. Fruit from the estate is complementary.

**LL-AL  La Dauphine Estate**  *Map 1, J3, p205*  A four-bedroom Great House and two-bedroom Chateau Laffitte on a 200-acre plantation 5 miles from Soufrière (see Villa Beach Cottages p.94 for contact details). Built in 1890 in gingerbread style, surrounded by lush gardens and hills, the houses have recently been refurbished to modern standards, and a housekeeper/cook is provided. Good hiking along nature trails and through the fruit plantation.

**L-A  La Haut Plantation**, 1½ miles north of Soufrière, **T** 4597008, www.lahaut.com  *Map 1, H2, p205*  This small hotel, restaurant and bar has only seven rooms, of which the cheapest in a cottage has the best view from its large balcony. The others, in an attractive, West-Indian style building, are small and uninspiring, although perfectly comfortable. The restaurant and pool have tremendous views over Soufrière, the Pitons and the Caribbean Sea.

**L-B  Humming Bird Beach Resort**, **T** 4597232, www.istlucia.co.uk.  *Map 1, H2, p205*  In a convenient location at the north end of the bay right on the beach and within walking distance of the town, the resort has 10 rather dark but good-value rooms and a hillside cottage across the road, a restaurant with a good view and a bar with no view, a batik studio and a pool.

**AL-C  The Still Plantation and Beach Resort**, **T** 4597261, www.thestillresort.com  *Map 1 H2 and I3 p205*  One resort, two locations. Inland on a 400-acre working **plantation** but within walking distance of the town, there are apartments and studios with a huge restaurant often used by tour parties but only open for breakfast and lunch. The rooms are vast and comfortable although not fancy, and excellent value for families or groups. Kitchens are available. You can go hiking in the plantation and see how copra is made or visit the Old Water Wheel where there are bats. The **Beach Resort** really is right on the beach and rooms and the restaurant have a good view of the bay and Petit Piton.

**B Chez Camille**, 7 Bridge St, **T** 4595379, www.cavip.com/en/hotels/chezcamille.html  *Map 1, I2, p205*  This older style house with wrap-around balcony and St Lucian décor is clean and friendly with five rooms, family room available and a kitchen for guests' use or the maid can cook for you. A good restaurant attached where guests get 10% discount (does takeaways).

**D La Mirage Guesthouse**, **T** 4597010,  *Map 1, I2 p205*  English owner of Jamaican descent, Gilroy Lamontaigne, has four rooms which each sleep three, with bathroom, fan and fridge, lounge with cable TV and restaurant.

**D-E Home Guesthouse**, on the main square, **T** 4597318,  *Map 1, I2, p205*  A long-established basic hostelry, which can be noisy. Only cash accepted.

**E Peter Jackson** rents a double room, in his house on the edge of Soufrière, **T** 4597269  *Map 1, I2, p205*  Basic but good, full cooking facilities, Peter is friendly and helpful.

## Laborie

**A-B Mirage Beach**, on the west edge of the bay, **T** 4559763, www.cavip.com/mirage  *Map 1, I2, p205*  Five tasteful, cottage-style rooms with or without kitchenette, white walls and brightly coloured bedspreads and curtains, right on the beach hidden by palm trees, to the north of Laborie. The food is French and, where possible, organic fruit and vegetables from the garden or the market are used, along with fresh fish and lobster. Windsurfing, rainforest hikes or horse riding can be arranged. It is15 minutes by car to the airport.

## Camping

**Anse La Liberté**, **T** 4537656, www.slunatrust.org email natrust@candw.lc for bookings and rates  *Map 1, G2, p205*  The National Trust has opened a campsite here on a 133-acre site overlooking the bay just south of Canaries, with tents, raised wooden platforms or levelled bare sites, picnic tables and barbecues by each platform, cold water shower and toilet block. The black sand beach with good snorkelling is reached along a hot path through the bush, down a ladder. Other trails lead through the dry tropical vegetation. A central open-sided building, called the Bro Iyee Hippolyte Community Centre, has an unobstructed view of the west coast and is a fantastic place from which to watch the sunset. The guardian sleeps here when there are campers. The road to the office and the short cut road to the campsite are both atrocious and 4WD or at least high clearance is essential. You can also camp at **Fond d'Or,** contact Magdalene Joseph, **T** 4533242, but elsewhere camping is dangerous and there are no facilities.

## Villa rental

Villa rental is increasingly popular in St Lucia and self-catering accommodation is available throughout the island. Some agencies to try include:
**Caribbean Villas**, **T** 866-2732563 in the USA, also offices in the UK and Canada, www.caribbeanvillas.org;
**Caribbean Way**, **T** 514-3933003 in the USA, http://st-lucia.caribbeanway.com;

**Forever Summer Villas**, **T** 1-888-4092575,
www.foreversummer.net;
**Gateway Villas**, **T** 01758-4508611 in the UK,
www.gatewayvillas.org;
**Goin2Travel**, www.going2travel.com;
**Holiday Rentals**, www.holiday-rentals.co.uk;
**Tropical Villas**, **T** 758-4508240 in St Lucia, www.tropicalvillas.net;
**Unusual Villa and Island Rentals**, **T** 804-2882623,
www.unusualvillarental.com;
**Villas Caribe**, **T** 303-6803100, http://stlucia.villascaribe.com

Eating and drinking

The local style of cooking is known as Creole and is a mixture of all the cultural influences of the island's immigrants over the centuries, from starchy vegetables to sustain African slaves to gourmet sauces and garnishes dating from the days when the French governed the island. The movement of people along the chain of Caribbean islands means that you can also find *rotis* from Trinidad and *jerk* from Jamaica, although these have been adapted from what you can expect on those islands. Fish and seafood are plentiful, fresh and delicious, but make sure you only eat lobster and conch in season (September-April) to avoid overfishing.

The standard of cooking in restaurants is high and there are several well-respected chefs practising their art. Hotels and restaurants will offer you a selection of international and local dishes using ingredients grown in the region, but for really authentic Creole food you should try local cafeterias and street vendors.

**Eating codes**

Price

| | |
|---|---|
| ⅢⅢⅢ | US$20 and over |
| ⅢⅢ | US$10-20 |
| Ⅲ | US$10 and under |

Prices refer to the cost of a main course. Service is usually 10%.

A local speciality is **accra,** a deep-fried fish-cake made of salted cod, an ingredient also used in saltfish and green fig, where the fig is actually green banana. There is a wide range of tropical fruit and vegetables on offer and it is worth strolling round the market to see what everything looks like before it ends up on your plate.

**Breadfruit**, called *bwapen* in Kwéyòl, is a large, round, starchy fruit which grows on huge trees brought to the islands by Captain Bligh of the *Mutiny on the Bounty* fame. These are usually eaten fried or boiled and have been a staple for centuries.

**Christophene** is another local vegetable which can be prepared in many ways, but is delicious baked in a cheese sauce. **Dasheen** is a root vegetable with green leaves, rather like spinach, which are used to make the tasty and nutritious callaloo soup. **Plantains** are eaten boiled or fried as a savoury vegetable, while green bananas, known as **figs**, can be cooked before they are ripe enough to eat raw as a fruit. Breakfast buffets are usually groaning under the weight of tropical fruits, from the bananas, pineapples, melons, oranges and grapefruit to mango, of which there are nearly 100 varieties, papaya/pawpaw (*papay* in Kwéyòl), sugar apple, soursop, sweetsop, carambola and love apple.

There are about ten good-value local eateries in the street adjoining the central market in Castries, with tables outside, offering heaped plates of local food, at lunchtime only. A standard meal of meat, plantains, potatoes, macaroni, rice and lettuce, washed down with a glass of passion-fruit juice, costs around EC$10. Vendors outside *Julian's* at Gablewoods Mall sometimes sell home-made cassava bread and a local delicacy called *permi* made of cornmeal and coconut wrapped up in a banana leaf. For other foods such as bakes, floats, fish, chicken, dal rotis (split pea), be sure that they are freshly cooked for the best flavour. The best places for freshly caught **seafood**, cooked to your specification, are the street parties at Anse La Raye, Dennery and Vieux Fort, where local fishermen sell their catch to be cooked on huge oil drum barbecues. If you prefer the international style of fast food, you can find burgers, pizzas and fried chicken in Castries and Rodney Bay.

You can get a snack at any time of day at a beach bar but most places open for **breakfast** from 0800-1000, **lunch** from1200-1400 and **dinner** from1800-2200. Hotels often start breakfast earlier, particularly if they are catering for an active crowd, such as divers, who need to be on the boat by 0900. Breakfast is usually served buffet style with croissants, pastries and fruit. Some restaurants will stay open at night late if they have a bar attached or there is live entertainment, but the kitchen usually closes by 2300.

Like most islands, St Lucia has its own **rum**, produced by St Lucia Distillers. Rums range from strong white to smooth dark and there are several brands on the shelves (see p129, but they are mostly used for mixing in cocktails. Rum-based liqueurs are also produced, such as the coffee flavoured *Ti Tasse*, which is great on ice cream if you don't want to drink it neat. The local **beer** is Piton, brewed in Vieux Fort and drunk very cold for maximum refreshment. A shandy on St Lucia is a mixture of beer and ginger ale; if it's a **Piton shandy** it can be with lemon or sorrel. The usual variety of carbonated soft drinks is available, sometimes imported, sometimes locally bottled. In Castries cold drinks are sold on street corners, EC$1 for a coke, drink it and return the bottle. **Coconut water** sold by vendors is always refreshingly cool and sterile. Coconuts are picked unripe when they are full of water. Other local soft drinks include **tamarind**, a bitter sweet drink made from the pods of the tamarind tree.

# Castries

## The Centre

**Ψ¶-Ψ Great Enterprise**, on Mongiraud, **T** 4530893. *Adjacent to the S&S building. Mon-Sat 1100-2130, Sun and holidays 1730-2130 Map 2, G2, p206* Chinese fast food, popular at lunchtimes with several stir-fry dishes at the counter or à la carte menu with an extensive selection of seafood, meat and vegetable dishes. Eat in or takeaway. Clean and pleasant, friendly service.

**Ψ Chung's**, John Compton Highway, **T** 4521499. *Opposite the playing field. 1100-2000 or so. Map 2, B3, p206* Pleasant, with inexpensive good food and a set menu of soup and three choices and coffee. MSG is used in a few dishes but if you don't want it, say so. They will also cater for allergies, such as wheat.

**Ψ Flamingo**, William Peter Blvd. *Open until about 1600, closes about 1200 on Sat. Map 2, G3, p206* Favourite local place for a cheeseburger (EC$6.50) or roti; for a chicken roti, specify you want it without skin and bones.

**Ψ Kimlans**, Derek Walcott Square, **T** 4521136. *Mon-Sat, 0700-2300. Map 2, G3, p206* A chicken and potato roti, washed down with a local juice, overlooking the square, will renew your energy for sightseeing in this cheap upstairs café and bar with veranda. A good place for people-watching.

## Vigie

**Ψ¶¶-Ψ¶ Coal Pot**, at Vigie Marina, **T** 4525566. *Lunch and dinner except Sat when dinner only, closed Sun. Map 2, C0, p206* The place to eat, outstanding, reservations essential. A very romantic, candlelit interior with beautiful artwork or a terrace overlooking the marina are the settings for sophisticated international cuisine. Delicious fresh food with all the trimmings is accompanied by a good wine list.

¶¶¶-¶¶ **Froggie Jack's**, at Vigie Cove, **T** 4581900, www.froggiejacques.com *Lunch Mon-Fri from 1100 and dinner Mon-Sat from 1900, bar open Mon-Sat from 1830.* *Map 2, C1, p206* Waterfront bistro, open-air dining in a garden with French and Caribbean cuisine, beautifully presented. Try their home-smoked local fish or salsa with breadfruit chips. Run by former executives at Anse Chastanet and Jalousie, with French chef, Jack Rioux.

¶ **En Bas Bwapen Créole Kitchen**, **T** 4521971. *Behind a fence at the bend in the Castries to Gros Islet road as it runs by the airport runway. Breakfast and lunch.* *Map 2, B3, p206* Very local place offering good, filling Creole cooking. Most expensive meal EC$10.

¶ **Friends at Casa Vigie**, first floor. *Just below the Venezuelan embassy. Mon-Thu, Fri 1000-2400, Sat 1000-1800.* *Map 1, C3, p204* Attractive patisserie and café serving very good sandwiches. Lovely walk from here to the Vigie lighthouse.

## Morne Fortune

¶¶ **Bon Appetit**, Top of the Morne, **T** 452275. *Lunch and dinner.* *Map 1, D4, p204* Excellent daily specials and spectacular views down to Castries. International food using local ingredients, delicious seafood crêpes and lots of fish. The chef is French and her husband, who is Italian, waits at table. It is very small, with only five tables, so reservations advised. Also rooms available, see p93.

¶¶ **The Green Parrot**, Top of the Morne, **T** 4523399. *Lunch and dinner.* *Map 1, D4, p204* Four-course dinner US$37, serves

### ★ Cheap eats

**Best**

- Anse La Raye fish fry on Fridays, p73
- Dennery fish-on-the-beach at weekends, p59
- En Bas Bwapen Créole Kitchen, p114
- The Wall, p119
- Castries central market vendors, p36

excellent lunches daily, with lots of Caribbean specialities and a good selection of tropical vegetables. Have a cocktail in the lounge before dinner – the chairs are worth it alone. Shows on Wednesday and Saturday; *Ladies' Night* Monday when you get two dinners for the price of one (dress smartly, the waiters are in tuxedos).

# North to Rodney Bay and Gros Islet

## Gablewoods Mall

♟♟-♟ **Miss Saigon**, Gablewoods Mall, **T** 4517309. *Breakfast, lunch and dinner, open daily. Map 1, C4, p204* Serves full English breakfast for EC$18, Chinese and Oriental food for other meals. St Lucians who work in the area come here for lunch.

♟ **BJ's Pepper Pot**, Marisule, **T** 4501030. *Along the main road. Tue-Sat, from 1100. Map 1, B4, p204* Jamaican cooking with jerk food to get you sweating and pepper pot, prices up to EC$18.

♟ **The Wharf**, Choc Bay, **T** 4504844 *Short distance past Gablewoods Mall. 0900-2400, happy hour 1800-1900 daily. Map 1, B4, p204* Beach setting, sandwiched between the road and the sea, waiter service to your sunbed. A varied menu, reasonable prices, beer EC$5-6, house wine EC$6, BLT EC$12, hamburger

EC$15. Lively in the evenings, restaurant, bar and dancing, karaoke Wednesday and Friday nights, soul, salsa and smooch Thursday with *Ladies' Night* after 2100, live music Saturdays, brunch on Sundays.

## Rodney Bay

**♥♥♥-♥♥ Buzz**, opposite Royal St Lucia, **T** 4580450, www.buzzstlucia. com *1700-late, closed Mon in summer, Sun brunch in season Map 3, E5, p207* Seafood and grill with a mixture of local and international dishes, lobster, lamb, pepperpot and vegetarian dishes. **The** place to be, very popular with the in-crowd and reservations are recommended unless you are prepared to wait an hour or more. Indoor or outdoor seating; even indoors is very open and airy with the shutters raised, blue and lemon yellow décor in West-Indian style building – smart but comfortable.

**♥♥♥-♥♥ Charthouse**, overlooking the lagoon, by Reduit Beach, **T** 4528115, www.charthousestlucia.com *Mon-Sat 1800-2230. Map 3, F5, p207* Open-air restaurant, a room without walls overlooking the yachts, known for its prime US beef, particularly the roast rib and excellent rib steak, as well as lobster and seafood.

**♥♥ Big Chef**, Just round the bend from Shamrock, **T** 4500210. *Mon-Sat from 1800. Map 3, F5, p207* Owner/chef of this popular steak house, Peter Kouly from Denmark is a local character of note.

**♥♥ Capone's Piazza**, **T** 4520284. *Tue-Sun 1100-2400. Map 3, F5, p207* A very pleasant place to come for pizza and pasta of recently improved quality with good service. Eat on the terrace or in the garden. Right in the centre of the strip and convenient for going on to a club or bar. Inside Capone's is now a night club, the *Green Room*, (*Wed-Sat from 1900*) with a pianist followed by other musicians who usually arrive around 2100.

♏ **Eagles Inn**, at the entrance to Rodney Bay Marina, **T** 4520650. *1000-0200. Map 3, E6, p207* You can sit on the terrace for lunch and watch the boats go by and enjoy good and not too expensive cuisine. Dinner is served upstairs. Great fish.

♏ **Key Largo**, on highway, past Julian's supermarket, **T** 4520282. *Next to Aquatic Centre in a two-storey building with Sportivo upstairs. Map 3, F6, p207* Good pizza from a wood-fired oven.

♏ **Memories of Hong Kong**, opposite Royal St Lucian hotel, **T/F** 4528218. *Mon-Sat 1700-2230. Map 3, E5, p207* A breezy location with fairy lights and lanterns around the veranda, a Chinese chef from Hong Kong, good food and plenty of it. Crispy aromatic duck could be a bit crispier and the pancakes lighter.

♏ **Scuttlebutts**, at the marina, **T** 4520351, VHS Channel 68. *0730-2400 or later. Map 3, E6, p207* Right on the water, with nautical decoration and offering an extensive menu of salads, pasta, ribs, chicken, steak, chilli and an all-day breakfast menu. On-board catering and provisioning packs for yachties as well as a dinghy dock and takeaway service. Lively atmosphere and stays open as long as there are clients; TV screens for sport, internet access, pool and pool bar, barbecue, lawn area with five-a-side games.

♏ **Spinnakers**, directly on the beach at Reduit, **T** 4528491. *Breakfast, lunch and dinner daily, happy hour 1800-1900. Map 3, E5, p207* Full English breakfast for EC$26 in an excellent location, though food and service suffer when it is busy; good too for coffee and desserts and they also hire out loungers for EC$5 per day.

♏ **The Cat's Whiskers**, just by Spinnakers, **T** 4528880. *Tue-Sun 0800-2300. Map 3, E5, p207* Also known as the English Pub. Traditional English pub food, Sunday roast beef and Yorkshire pudding, steak and kidney pie, Cornish pasties.

**The Lime**, T 4520761. *1100 till late, closed Tue.  Map 3, F5, p207*  Serves steak cooked over a charcoal grill, fish, shrimp, lobster, rotis and snacks at moderate prices in a friendly atmosphere. Good portions, nothing fancy.

**Tilly's 2x4**, on the highway, T 4584440.  *Just past Key Largo, entrance from road on foot but around the back by car.  1000-2400, happy hour 1700-1900.  Map 3, F7, p207*  Like an old chattel house and rum shop, serving lots of fish, grilled or baked or Creole, with side dishes of Caribbean vegetables and a great rum punch.

**Razmataz**, opposite Royal St Lucian, T/F 4529800.  *Open from 1600, happy hour 1700-1900, closed Thu.  Map 3, E5, p207*  Indian restaurant with a chef from Nepal, serving a wide range of dishes. A friendly place and if you're still around after happy hour, John plays guitar and sings romantic songs from the 60s and 70s, or on Saturday a belly dancer weaves her way around the diners.

**The Villa**, up on the hill at Caribbean Jewel Beach Resort, T 4529199.  *0730-2300.  Map 3, F4, p207*  Fabulous view over Rodney Bay and a good lunch-time spot for sitting on the balcony and watching the world down there. The international menu offers burgers, salads, fish and various entrées with rice or chips. On Friday night they do a very cheap barbecue from 1800 for only EC$10 for chicken, EC$15 for fish, a bargain and very popular.

**Breadbasket**, at the marina, T 4520647.  *Mon-Sat 0700-1700, Sun 0600-1300.  Map 3, E6, p207*  A favourite for breakfast. Fantastic home-made bread, great rotis and pastries. Very good value.

**Elena's ice cream parlour**, Rodney Bay village, T 4580576.  *Mon, Wed-Fri 0900-2300, Sat-Sun 0900-2400.  Map 3, F5, p207*  At tables under umbrellas outside in a small courtyard, you can sample home-made ice cream and local fruit sorbets, good cappuccino and snacks; there is also another outlet at the Marina called *Café Olé*, open from 0700.

## Gros Islet

🍴 **Milo's**, next door to Anette's (see p99), **T** 4500098. *Mon-Sat 0900-2200. Map 1, A5, p204* Milo is a super host and prices are medium for the area in this new, very good restaurant in a colonial house. Creole food to order.

🍴 **La Panache**, Cas-en-Bas Rd, **T** 4500765, augustinh@candw.lc *Map 1, A5, p204* Restaurant attached to the guesthouse, see p99, run by Henry Augustin. Breakfast daily US$3-8, and a few nights a week he cooks tasty Creole dinners (Henry's grandmother's recipes) US$13, by reservation only. Everyone sits around a large table and bowls of chicken, fish, christophene and other vegetables are passed around, family style. There is a bar with excellent alcoholic and non-alcoholic cocktails, but don't expect a great wine list. Ask if you can take your own if its important.

🍴 **The Wall**, corner of Marie Thérèse and Dauphin streets, **T** 4500338. *Mon-Sat 0700-2300, much later on Fri. Map 3, D5, p207* Excellent value at US$4.50 for a huge plateful. Rooms also available, see p100.

## Pigeon Island

🍴 **Jambe de Bois**, **T** 4580728/4520321. *From breakfast until 2130. Map 3, B4, p207* A very pleasant location at the water's edge within stone walls in the style of the military buildings, under a thatched roof, with rustic, wooden furniture and seating outside or inside. Serves reasonably priced meals, baguettes, fish, soup, salads and cakes, and offers an art gallery, book swap, post cards and internet access at EC$20 per hr.

♥♥-♥ **Captain's Cellar Pub and Oscar's Restaurant**, T 4500918, thecaptainscellarpub@hotmail.com  *Wed-Mon 1000-2300 or later, Tue 1000-1700.  Map 3, B4, p207*  Underneath the Interpretation Centre, with tables outside with view over the channel and Burgot Rocks, or in the original Captain's cellar where provisions were stored. Watch your head, the arches are very low. Very atmospheric and they claim there's a ghost. Open for breakfast and lunch in the pub daily, then dinner in Oscar's alongside  with simple dishes such as burgers, roti, chilli, curries, salads and fish. Bottled and draught Piton and other beers. Free entry to Pigeon Island after 1700.

# The north and northeast coasts

## Cap Estate

♥♥♥ **The Great House Restaurant**, T 4500450, greathouse@clubstlucia.com  *Tue-Sun, tea 1630-1730, happy hour 1730-1830, dinner 1830-2145.  Map 3, A6, p207*  Traditional tea followed by happy hour sunset watching. Dinner is expensive, eat à la carte or Great House menu EC$100. A Great House has been standing here since the 18th century, inhabited by the de Longueville proprietors of the Cap Estate and variously destroyed by Brigands and hurricanes. Today's restaurant emulates the grand living of plantation owners, but the grounds could do with clearance of litter.

# East coast to Vieux Fort

## East coast

♥♥ **Whispering Palm**, Foxgrove Inn, Mon Repos, T 4553800, www.foxgroveinn.com  *Breakfast, lunch and dinner.  Map 1, H6, p205*  Good food and a spectacular view from the balcony of the restaurant over Praslin Bay and the Atlantic Ocean. Try the smoked fish or smoked duck salad for a delicious lunch, washed down with local juice such as guava or passion-fruit. Main dishes include fish, steak or pasta. A great place to stop during a tour of the east coast.

�♌ **Manje Domi**, Desruisseaux, **T** 4550729, manje-domi@candw.lc *Map 1, J6, p205* Guest house and restaurant run by Kenny G deep in the countryside, offering local food with Creole, curry or ginger sauces, all freshly prepared, vegetarian meals on request. Dinner, bed and breakfast is less than US$100 per couple, see p100.

## Vieux Fort

�♌ **Juliette's Lodge**, Beanfield, Vieux Fort, **T** 4545300, www.julietteslodge.com *Down a road opposite the entrance to the airport. Breakfast, lunch and dinner. Map 1, L6, p205* Hotel restaurant with view of runway, Maria Islands and lighthouse from the hillside, convenient for the beach too. Simple menu with fish, meat, burgers, salads, omelettes, sandwiches and pasta.

� **Pointe Sable Beach Resort** (formerly Sandy Beach), Anse de Sables, **T** 4546002. *A bit further down from Reef, on the beach and on the highway. Open all day until the last guest leaves. Map 1, L6, p205* Beach bar in an excellent location, a delightful stopping place with good food, if a little overpriced. Have a swim and lunch.

♌ **The Annex**, close to Hewanorra Airport, **T** 4546200. *Mon-Fri 0900 to midnight, Sat-Sun, 1000-0200. Map 1, L6, p205* Good local food. One of the best places within walking distance of the airport for drinks, meal or a swim if you are passing time before a flight.

♌ **The Reef**, at Anse de Sables beach, **T** 4543418. *Breakfast, lunch and dinner. Map 1, L6, p205* Owned by Cecile Wiltshire, this pleasant bar serves local drinks and delicacies, milk shakes and

**★ Waterfront dining**

**Best**

• Jambe de Bois, Pigeon Island, p119
• Scuttlebutts, Rodney Bay Marina, p117
• Old Courthouse, Soufrière, p124
• Froggie Jack's, Vigie, p114
• Chateau Mygo, Marigot Bay, p122

cocktails, seafood, fish and chips, burgers and baguettes, at reasonable price. There are tables out by the beach under sea grape trees as well as inside the building. Internet café.

# West coast to Soufrière and the Pitons

## Marigot Bay

♉ **Chateau Mygo**, **T** 4514772, www.chateaumygo.com *0700-2300. Map 1, E3, p204* Waterfront bar and grill serving traditional hot bakes and cocoa tea for breakfast, Tuesday night steak, US$12, with music and dancing on the beach, thin crust pizzas from US$8, credit cards accepted and reservations advised. Gift shop, phone cards available and car rental.

♉ **JJ's Restaurant and Bar**, **T** 4514076. *1000 till late. Map 1, E3, p204* Cheaper than many hotels in the bay JJ's specializes in fresh local dishes, reasonably priced crayfish, crab and lobster: Wednesday night crabs and a live band, Friday salsa, Saturday live band.

♉ **Rainforest Hideaway**, **T** 2860511. *Breakfast, lunch and dinner. Map 1, E3, p204* Newly opened and part of the Discovery condo construction project, it is right by the old Seahorse jetty and reached by the ferry boat, EC$5 return, refundable at restaurant.

Ⓨ **Shack Bar & Grill**, **T** 4514145. *Mon-Fri from 1500, Sat-Sun from 1200, happy hour 1700-1900, dinner 1830-2200. Map 1, E3, p204* Built over the water with a tie-up for dinghies, and serving burgers, steaks and seafood. Reservations are recommended for dinner.

---

## Soufrière

ⓎⓎⓎ **Dasheene**, at Ladera Resort, **T** 4597323. *Breakfast for hotel guests only, lunch 1130-1430, and dinner 1830-2130. Map 1, I12, p205* Up on a hillside, 1,000 feet above sea level with wonderful views of the Pitons – worth coming here for, even if only for a drink. The good food, light and modern Caribbean Creole, features fresh local produce as well as some international delicacies. Chef Nigel Mitchel invites chefs from abroad for the season to design innovative and eclectic daily menus.

ⓎⓎ-Ⓨ **Mango Tree**, Stonefield Estate Villa Resort, **T** 4597037, www.stonefieldvillas.com *0730-2200. Map 1, I12, p205* Gorgeous setting overlooking Petit Piton and Malgrétoute beach, great for watching the sun set. Serving breakfast, lunch and dinner, the menu is varied and wide ranging, with some vegetarian dishes as well as the usual seafood, meat and pasta. A barbecue on Thursdays with live music is usually heavily booked, so even guests have to make reservations.

ⓎⓎ-Ⓨ **The Humming Bird**, **T** 4597232. *Open from 0700 Map 1, H2, p205* A nice place to take a swim and eat with a view of the town and Petit Piton. A good but expensive varied menu features French, Creole and seafood dishes, with daily specials and lunchtime salads and sandwiches. The barman is a great fund of information on horoscopes. See also p105

♥♥ **The Old Courthouse**, T 4595002. *Open daily. Map 1, I2, p205* Bar, restaurant and batik gallery. Waterfront dining on French Creole and Southeast Asian dishes in a building dating from 1898. Credit cards accepted. A lovely setting and good view but it can be noisy.

♥♥ **The Still**, Soufrière Road, T 4597224. *0800-1700. Map 1, I3, p205* The restaurant has a great view of Petit Piton and the bay and is not cheap but serves local vegetables grown on site. Most dinner main courses cost US$19-23, with fish at the low end and steak the high, surf'n'turf US$36. A lunch menu offers sandwiches, salads, vegetarian dishes, seafood and grills. See Sleeping, p143.

♥♥-♥ **La Haut Plantation**, on the west coast road, T 4597008, www.lahaut.com *1 ½ miles north of Soufrière. 0800-1100, 1200-1600, 1700-2100. Map 1, H2, p205* Excellent lunch with some unusual items such as pumpkin chips, crêpes and rotis. Dinner is also delicious with a good wine list. Stunning views of Pitons and Sulphur Springs, seven bedrooms (see Sleeping p ) and a huge TV in the sports bar.

♥ **Jalam's**, Market St. *Map 1, I2, p205* A pleasant rasta eating place run by Jalam, in a wooden house up a couple of steps from street level, small, clean, cheap, EC$10 for a dal, a roti and two fresh juices.

♥ **Purity Bakery**, *Near the church in the main square. Map 1, I2, p205* Serves breakfast with good coffee, rolls and cakes.

♥ **The Barbican restaurant and bar**, Étangs Soufrière, T 4597888. *On the road to Vieux Fort. Map 1, J3, p205* A clean and popular restaurant, run by the very welcoming Mr and Mrs Smith who offer local food at local prices and good home cooking.

Most of St Lucia's nightlife revolves around the hotels, while some restaurants host live bands. The choice varies from steel bands, jazz groups, folk dancing, crab racing, fire eating and limbo dancers. The hotels welcome guests from outside, but this might not be the authentic St Lucia experience you are looking for. Bars and clubs are concentrated around Rodney Bay, all within easy walking distance of each other. Some have strict entry restrictions on age and dress, so check beforehand. They offer a mix of live bands and DJs playing regional and international music.

For more informal entertainment there are street parties. Friday nights are big for going out and St Lucians enjoy eating fresh local food while socialising in the open air, known as *liming*, followed by music and dancing, known as a *jump-up*.

The highlight of the week is currently **Seafood Friday**, at **Anse La Raye**, just south of Castries, where you can get the cheapest and freshest lobster on the island in season and fish at any time of year. The entire street running parallel to the bay has chairs and tables under awnings, serving seafood of your choice. However, it is so popular that food tends to run out by 2100, so get there early. Everyone is very friendly and there is no hassling. Music is at a bearable pitch and sometimes you can hear a local quadrille band. If you are on the east coast, you can try **Dennery** for **fish-on-the-beach** at weekends, 1600-0200, while **Sware**, Vieux Fort, is a lively **Friday street party** where you can eat unlimited fish accompanied by the beat of local music.

Later on, head for the **jump-up** from 2200 at **Gros Islet** (see 48), where it is hard to resist getting involved. If you haven't eaten beforehand, or if you work up another appetite, you can get barbecued chicken legs, lambi/conch, accra (fish cakes) and floats from the street stalls. The mix of tourists to St Lucians is weighted heavily towards the former, but it can be enjoyable nonetheless if you are a night owl who likes music and dancing. There can be more hassling here and you should stay away from anyone offering drugs.

**Sunset cruises** are a good way of winding down after a busy day on the beach. Boats usually travel down the west coast and serve champagne, rum cocktails or soft drinks to help you spot the elusive green flash as the sun dips below the horizon, see Tours, p28.

# Rodney Bay

## Bars

**Green Room**, Capone's, **T** 4520003. *Wed-Sat, 1900-late.* *Map 3, F5, p207* Art décor wine bar with a/c, comfy sofas and piano music, followed by other musicians who get there around 2100. Good wine by the glass or great non-alcoholic 'power' drinks. La Piazza restaurant outside for pizzas and pasta, see p116

**Happy Day Bar**, next to and part of Eagles Inn, T 4520650. *1000-0200.* *Map 3, E6, p207* Gives two drinks for the price of one all day, clumsy system of vouchers for the second drink, lots of hassling of unaccompanied women.

**Rumours**, opposite Scotia Bank, **T** 4529249. *Open from 1730.* *Map 3, F5, p207* Bar, restaurant (also open for lunch *Mon-Fri 1130-1430*), pool tables, dance floor. Wednesday night is Latin night when the Cuban medical staff from the polyclinic come out to salsa. Great fun and very energetic. The cockney salsa trainer, Ken, gives free lessons. Tuesday is karaoke and Thursday-Saturday Marcus and DJ Play provide club music. Entry fee of EC$10 after 2300 unless you have a VIP card.

**Triangle Pub**, across from *The Lime*, **T** 4520334. *Open daily 1100-late.* *Map 3, B4, p207* Local food and barbecue, eat in or take out, live bands, pan, jazz.

## Clubs

**Charlie's Late Night Club**, Rodney Bay village, **T** 4580565. *Map 3, F5, p207* A big yellow building containing *Charlie's Boutique* selling stylish clothing, shoes, open 1000-2200, the *Courtyard Café*, with an

### Spice Rum

One of the biggest sellers is *Denros*, or *Strong Rum*, 80% alcohol and one of the strongest overproof rums in the Caribbean. It is the base for most of the spiced rum sold on St Lucia, so treat with caution. Rum shops stock 5-gallon plastic containers of the stuff, combining it with fruits and spices and calling it 'spice'. The premium white rum is *Bounty Crystal White Rum*, 40% alcohol, which is the basis of the rum cocktails served in tourist bars and hotels. There is an amber *Bounty Rum*, which is also used in cocktails and is cheaper than imported rum from other islands. *Old Fort Reserve Rum* is the smoothest, the *Chairman's Reserve* has recently won an international award, while *Kwéyòl Spice Rum* is a *bois bande* (bark) spice rum.

There is nothing better at the end of a busy day than finding a pleasant spot overlooking the sea with a rum in your hand to watch the sunset and look out for the green flash. The theory is that the more rum you drink, the more likely you are to see this flash of green on the horizon as the sun goes down.

Italian menu for coffee, brunch and lunch, the *Piano Bar*, with comfy seating and live or taped music, the *Olive Garden Restaurant*, also Italian, open in the evenings, and *Charlie's Late Night Club*. On Wednesday there is a salsa and zouk party, Thursday is 70s, 80s and 90s music, Friday is the DJ Shane, Saturday a jam and DJ, and Sunday, the *Lyric Café*, with poetry, spoken work and live acoustics.

**Upper Level Nite Club**, upstairs at *The Lime*, **T** 4520761 *Tue, Fri, Sat until late. Map 3, F5, p207* Popular place for those who just want to hang out. Live music, karaoke and food. Sometimes has special events with a cover charge.

# Pigeon Island

---

**Bars**

**Captain's Cellar Pub**, **T** 4500918,
thecaptainscellarpub@hotmail.com  *Wed-Mon 1000-2300 or later,
Tue 1000-1700.  Map 3, B4, p207*  Underneath the Interpretation
Centre, with tables outside with good view over the channel and
Burgot Rocks, or in the original Captain's cellar where provisions
were stored. Watch your head, the arches are very low. Very
atmospheric and they claim there's a ghost. Bottled and draught
Piton and other beers. Free entry to Pigeon Island after 1700.

**Jambe de Bois**,**T** 4580728/4520321.  *Map 3, B4, p207*  On Sun
evening there is a jazz group, around 1830-2130, very pleasant to
sit at the tables on the deck at the water's edge.

# Marigot Bay

---

**Clubs**

**JJ's Paradise**, **T** 4514076.  *Open until very late.  Map 1, E3, p204*
Casual, good mixture of locals and tourists, live, loud Caribbean
music at weekends in simple disco, Friday can be very busy,
Saturday pleasantly so, happy hour all night. Wednesday is
Seafood Night, which is so popular that reservations are required.
Frequent shows, karaoke, taxi service can be arranged.

St Lucia hasn't got a huge arts scene as its culture has developed in other ways. While there are major poets and playwrights on the island (such as the Nobel Laureate Derek Walcott) and everybody loves music and dance, theatre as such is rather ad hoc or geared to specific festivals, usually on an annual basis. There are shows: concerts, drama, dance, comedy, at the National Cultural Centre (Castries), the Light House Theatre (Tapion) and occasionally at the Great House Theatre (Cap Estate). They can give you a better taste of St Lucian culture than hotel shows. The Festival of Comedy, see p139, is a major fundraiser but there is nothing permanent.

Live music and dance can be found in bars and clubs in the Rodney Bay area several nights a week, when you might find an established band or a new group testing the waters. Hotels also lay on entertainment and are a frequent venue for steel pan music, folk dancing and mock carnival singing and dancing. The big event though is the annual St Lucia Jazz Festival in May, now one of the most important music festivals in the Caribbean calendar.

# Cinema

There is no home grown cinema industry, although **Jako Productions** is a small company branching out into film and music video production as well as publishing. St Lucia is occasionally used for film locations. Marigot Bay featured in *Dr Doolittle*, and *Water* was also filmed here. Ladera Resort was used for the filming of *Superman II*. The **St Lucia Film Commission** is on the 3rd floor, Ministry of Tourism, Castries, **T** 4684620.

**Cinema 2000**, on the main road in Rodney Bay.   *Above Julian's supermarket. Map 3 F6, p207*  Entrance upstairs where there are pool tables, car/bike racing computer machines, a bar with tables on the balcony and snacks. Tickets EC$15, but there are often special offers. There is a huge screen playing international releases, but the chaotic sound can blow you out of your seat. **Unique Taxi Service**, **T** 4520986, is based outside, *Vibes* music store  at the rear.

# Music

There is a good deal of French cultural influence here. Most of the islanders, who are predominantly of African descent, speak Kwéyòl, a similar language to French and the French Caribbean has also had an impact on music: you can hear zouk and cadance played as much as calypso and reggae.

**The Folk Research Centre** (see p39) has recorded local music. *Musical Traditions of St Lucia* has 32 selections representing all the musical genres, with information on the background of the various styles. *Lucian Kaiso* is an annual publication giving pictures and information on each season of St Lucian **calypso**. In the pre-Christmas period, small drum groups play in rural bars. Traditionally, singers improvise a few lines about people and events in the community and the public joins in. The singing is exclusively in Kwéyòl, wicked and full of sexual allusions.

## Musicians of St Lucia

St Lucia's most famous musician is **Luther Francois**, who plays a wide variety of instruments including guitar, bass, double bass, flute, saxophone, violin, piano and has played for every major local band: *Rasputin and the Mad Monks*, *Chapter Eight*, *Night Train*, *Tru Tones* and the *Luther Francois Quartet*.

He started St Lucia's first jazz workshop, and worked hard to improve local standards. He played with the *Wailers* and Peter Tosh and accompanied Tosh and Mick Jagger on sax. However, in the 1980s he moved to Martinique, where he experimented in the fusion of various Caribbean rhythms into jazz.

In 1988 he formed the first Caribbean-wide jazz band and their first album, *Morne du Don*, was recorded in Barbados in 1990.

Other local artistes to look out for include the veteran **Ronald 'Boo' Hinkson**, a musician, producer, arranger, composer and performer, who started out in the 1960s with the *Tru Tones*. When the band broke up he continued as a solo artist. He has written reggae, calypso, soca, R&B and blues songs for himself and others, but is currently leaning towards jazz, with a Caribbean bias.

**Carl Gustave** grew up in Los Angeles but returned to his St Lucian roots in the 1990s. He is a regular performer at the Jazz Festival and is a singer, songwriter and guitarist with elements of blues, R&B and funk.

**Rob 'Zi' Taylor** is a saxophonist and vocalist making his name on the music scene with his debut album, *Rise Up*, released in 2004 for the Jazz Festival www.zionsax.com.

There is usually something going on with frequent live performances by local or regional bands, but it is the annual **St Lucia Jazz Festival** in May which dominates the music scene drawing large crowds every year with lots of outdoor concerts. **Pigeon Island** is the venue for the top concerts. Most are open-air and take place in the evening, although fringe events are held anywhere, anytime, with local bands playing in Castries at lunchtime. If it rains, as it did in 2004, there is no alternative venue and concerts have to be cancelled. Both St Lucian and international musicians are invited and as well as jazz, played by international stars, you can hear Latin, salsa, soca and zouk, steel drums or Bob Marley. See p139 for details.

On a weekly basis, there is live and recorded music at the **Gros Islet jump-up**, while at the **Anse La Raye fish-fry** on a Friday night you can often catch a band playing the *Quadrille*, local folk dance music. *Country and Western* is a surprisingly big thing locally and can be found upstairs in Castries market on Friday nights.

# Theatre

**Derek Walcott Theatre**, at the *Great House*, Cap Estate **T** 4500450. *Map 3, A6, p207* An open-air theatre opened in 1995 but unfortunately not much used except for fundraising events and the Jazz Fest.

**La Sikwi**, Anse La Raye, *Map 1, F2, p204* Sikwi is Kwéyòl for sugar mill. There is a visit to the 150-year-old mill, followed by a full costume play reliving life in the village on a stage set into the hills with jazz bands and local acts. Gilland Adjhoda and his sons who organize events here can be contacted at the **Caribbean Hospitality Group**, **T** 4516511, **F** 4523714.

**The Gaiety**, Rodney Bay, **T** 4516511   *Map 3, F5, p207*   Also run by Mr Adjodha (see previous page), Arthur Miller's recent visit and recital was staged here and it is frequently used for visiting singers and musicians.

**National Cultural Centre**, Castries   *Map 2, D3, p206*   The NCC is an a/c auditorium which seats about 800. It comes under the auspices of the Ministry of Social Transformation, Culture and Local Government and can be rented for shows, plays, etc. It is often used for festivals such as the *Quadrille Festival* or the *Violin Festival*.

St Lucians are keen on their festivals and there are several celebrated throughout the year. These range from Carnival celebrations, sporting fixtures, music and cultural festivals and flower festivals. The event which draws most people, from outside the country as well as locals, is the May Jazz Festival, which is popular with musicians and audiences and has a good reputation so you need to make hotel bookings well in advance. International cricket matches also place a heavy burden on the island's accommodation, as these draw crowds from around the world, depending on who is playing. Carnival does not match up with that of Trinidad, but it is a colourful expression of traditional legends and competitions, great fun and a hot and sweaty experience if you join in with the dancing. St Lucia's cultural festivals are well worth looking out for, as they concentrate on the Creole/Kwéyòl heritage. The best example of this is *Jounen Kwéyòl* in October.

## January

The last week in the month is **Nobel Laureate Week** with lectures celebrating the two Nobel prize winners produced by the island. Both Sir Arthur Lewis and Derek Walcott were born on 23 January.

## February

**Independence Day** (22 February) is celebrated quite extensively. There is a large exhibition lasting several days from the various ministries, business and industry, and NGOs, such as the National Trust, and various sporting events, serious discussions, lectures and musical programmes. An annual **Quadrille Festival**, a national dress show is usually tied in to the Independence celebrations.

## March

The **Festival of Comedy** is held at the end of March at Pigeon Point (Cultural Centre if it is raining), organized by the St Lucia National Trust, **T** 4525005. Local and Caribbean storytellers and comedians come to entertain.

## May

The annual **St Lucia Jazz Festival** in May is now an internationally recognized event, drawing large crowds every year. Most concerts are open-air and take place in the evening, many on Pigeon Island, although fringe events are held anywhere, anytime, with local bands playing in Castries at lunchtime. As well as jazz, played by international stars, you can hear Latin, salsa, soca and zouk, steel drums or Bob Marley. For details **T** 4518566, www.stluciajazz.org. Tickets from US$35 or a season pass US$230. Contact the Department of Culture for programmes as shows are often poorly advertised. Tickets available at the Department of Culture and Sunshine Bookstore (Gablewoods Mall).

## June

On 29 June St Peter's Day is celebrated as the **Fisherman's Feast**, in which all the fishing boats are decorated.

## July

**Carnival** is a high point in the island's cultural activities, when colourful bands and costumed revellers make up processions through the streets. There is lots of music, dancing and drinking. Everything goes on for hours, great stamina is required to keep going. Carnival is now held in July, partly so as not to conflict with Trinidad's Carnival in February. Local writers, composers, singers and musicians produce biting social commentary in their calypsos. On the Saturday are the calypso finals, on Sunday the King and Queen of the band followed by J'ouvert at 0400 until 0800 or 0900. On Monday and Tuesday the official parades of the bands take place. Most official activities take place at Marchand Ground but warming-up parties and concerts are held all over the place. Tuesday night there is another street party. You can visit calypso 'tents' and 'jump' with a band, information from the Cultural Development Foundation, **T** 4521859, or www.stluciacarnival.com.

## August

1 August is **Emancipation Day** and **National Heroes Day** when St Lucia and other former British colonies celebrate the anniversary of the abolition of slavery.

The **Feast of the Rose of Lima** (*Fét La Wòz*) on 30 August is a big flower festival with local songs and dances.

## September

**St Lucia Bill Fishing Tournament**, a three-day competition for anglers from all over the Caribbean. Any fish weighing less than 250 lbs is tagged and returned to the sea. The weighing station is at Rodney Bay Marina.

## October

The **Feast of St Margaret Mary Alacoque** (*La Marguerite*) on 17 October is a rival flower festival to the one in August. Members of the societies gather in various public places around the island to dance and sing in costume.

The first Monday in October is **Thanksgiving**, held either to give thanks for no hurricane or for survival of a hurricane.

**Jounen Kwéyòl** (Creole Day) is on the last Sunday in October, although activities are held throughout the month and known as Creole Heritage Month. The Folk Research Centre, **T** 4522279, see p39, organizes a series of events. Four or five rural communities are selected for the celebration on Creole Day. There is local food, craft, music and different cultural shows. Expect traffic jams everywhere as people visit venues across the island. A lot is in Kwéyòl, but you will still have a good time and a chance to sample mouth-watering local food.

## November

**St Cecilia's Day** (22 November), is also known as **Musician's Day** (St Cecilia is the patron saint of music). Traditionally a small band of musicians would go around at daybreak playing a particular piece of music – not well received by those who had reached their beds late the night before.

December

**St Lucy's Day** (13 December), used to be called Discovery Day, but as Columbus' log shows he was not in the area at that time, it was renamed. It is now known as the **National Festival of Lights and Renewal**. St Lucy, the patron saint of light, is honoured by a procession of lanterns and the switching on the Christmas lights. For details contact Castries City Council, **T4** 522611 ext 7071.

**ARC** – Atlantic Rally for Cruisers. The world's largest trans-Atlantic crossing starts from Gran Canaria around 25 November and the first yacht usually arrives in the first week of December to lots of celebrations and parties.

**Christmas** is celebrated with sorrel, ginger beer, black pudding, black cake and calypso carols as well as most of the trappings of a British Christmas. Young men also enjoy hazardous cannon wars, a local custom where they cut lengths of large bamboo, hollow them out to the last nodule, prop them up like real cannon, make a small hole near the end and pour in kerosene. This is then lit with a stick and, as it vaporizes, there is an explosion of fuel and oxygen mixture with thunderous blasts of hot air and blinding flashes of light. Teams compete to see who can make the most noise and in quickest succession.

Castries market is essential to visit to see all the fruit, vegetables, spices, arts, crafts, clothing and other souvenirs that St Lucia has to offer. All your senses will be bathed in the colour, smells, tastes and noise of the place. If you are self-catering, this is a good place to buy your fruit and veg, but the supermarkets are well stocked so you won't need to come here frequently. Look out for roadside stands, which are good places to pick up bananas or local delicacies. There is a well-developed arts and crafts industry on the island and several highly respected local artists sell their work as well as many ex-pat artists who have chosen to base themselves here. It is best to bring all your reading needs with you as bookshops are not well stocked. St Lucians will appreciate any books you have finished with or you can donate them to a book swap.

## Arts and crafts

**Artsibit**, corner of Brazil and Mongiraud streets, T 4527865. *Mon-Fri 0900-1230, 1330-1700, Sat 1000-1200. Map 2, F3, p206* High-quality local crafts, pottery, sculpture, prints and paintings.

**Bagshaw's**, La Toc, T 4522139. *Mon-Fri 0830-1630, Sat 0830-1200. Map 1, C3, p204* Also shops at Marigot and Windjammer Landing. Very popular silk-screening studio. See p43.

**Caribbean Art Gallery**, Rodney Bay Marina, T 4528071, www.caribbeanartandantiques.com *Mon-Fri 0900-1700 Sat 0900-1300. Map 3, E6, p207* Llewellyn Xavier's gallery, see p187, with inexpensive framed prints and antique maps as well as his own work and that of local artists: water colours, oils, pen and ink, pencil drawings, limited-edition prints, hand-painted silk, collages, woodcuts, mixed media, art cards. Credit cards accepted, worldwide shipping with Fedex. Llewellyn Xavier has a second gallery, **Arts & Antiques** at Marigot Bay, T 4514150, same opening hours, and you can visit his studio, T 4509155 for an appointment.

**Caribelle Batik**, at Sea Island Cotton, Gablewoods Mall and Old Victoria Rd, The Morne and Bridge St. *Map 1, C4, p204* Batik fabrics and cotton clothing.

**Eudovics Art Studio**, in Goodlands, T 4522747. *Coming down from the Morne heading south. Map 1, D4, p204* Local handicrafts and beautiful large wood carvings.

**Harbour Gallery**, at the Pyramid, Pointe Seraphine, **T** 4560899. *Mon-Thu 0900-1600, Fri 0900-1400. Map 2, D1, p206* A fine showing of local artists, originals and prints. Limited edition Fine Art Giclée Prints by St Lucian artists, oli@caribbeangiclee.com. Print sizes range from 13" x 19" to 40" x 120" and cost from US$50.

**Inner Gallery**, Rodney Bay opposite Capone's, **T** 4528728, www.theinnergallery.com *Map 3, F5, p207* Exhibits the work of local artists including Arnold Toulon, Cedric George, Chris Cox, Nancy Cole, Sophie Barnard, Alcina Nolley, Jonathon Gladding.

**Lava Flow**, Pointe Seraphine and La Place Carenage, **T** 4525422, wildorchidstlucia@hotmail.com *Map 2, F3 and D1, p206* Hand painted ceramics and local pottery including the brightly painted bowls, servers and plates of Michelle Elliot.

**Sophie Barnard**, on the way to Gros Islet, **T** 4520946. *From Castries turn left just after the Texaco station. Mon-Fri 1000-1500. Map 1, B4, p204* Studio where masks and totems are carved from driftwood collected along the Atlantic coast or from discarded lumber off-cuts found in the forest. Prices from EC$140, also available from *Jambe de Bois* at Pigeon Island.

---

## Bookshops

**Book Salon**, Jeremie St on corner of Laborie St. *Map 2, F3, p206* Reasonable selection of paperbacks, several books on St Lucia, also stationery.

**Jambe de Bois**, on Pigeon Island. *Map 3, B4, p207* Also offers a book swap.

**Rodney Bay Shipping Services**, Rodney Bay  *Map 3, E6, p206*  Book exchange, two for one, mostly spy thrillers and light novels, not a huge selection, but useful.

**Sunshine Bookshop**, Gablewoods Mall (*Mon-Fri 0900-1745, Sat 0900-1630*), JQ Mall (*Mon-Sat 0900-1800, Sun 1000-1300*), and Pointe Seraphine (*Mon-Fri 0830-1630, Sat half day*).  *Map 1, C4, p204; Map 3 F5, p207; Map 2 D1, p206*  Books, foreign newspapers and magazines.

## Flowers

**Garden Gate Flowers**, Bois D'Orange, **T** 4529176, at Hewanorra, **T** 4547651, **F** 4529023.  *Map 1, B4, p204*  Takeaway boxes (cargo transport) and bouquets (hand luggage) of ginger, heliconia, anthuriums, 48 hours' notice required for export, US$12-30.

## Markets

Market day in **Castries** is Saturday and very picturesque. (It is much quieter on other days.) Those who speak Kwéyòl pay less than those who do not. A new public market has been built on the Castries waterfront, with the old market building renovated and turned into a craft market.  *Map 2, F3/4, p206*

● Buy a cocoa stick or 10 for US$5. To make hot chocolate, put two tablespoons of grated cocoa in a pan with half a pint of water and boil for 15 minutes, strain, then add dry milk, sugar, cinnamon and nutmeg to taste.

**Wire World**, booth 3, has charming figures by the award-winning Paulinus Clifford, **T** 4538727, also at Pointe Seraphine, he and the next artisan, Augustus Simon, a potter, **T** 4521507, will craft to order. Buy a coal-pot (native barbecue) for EC$12 and bring it home on your lap.

**Soufrière** has a market on the waterfront, as does **Anse La Raye** along the seafront road, with tourist stalls selling clothing and souvenirs and a fish market.

**Fisherman's Co-operative Market** on the John Compton Highway at the entrance to Pointe Seraphine. *Map 2, C2, p206* Fish is also sold by a Martiniquan woman inside the **public market**, good variety, hygienically displayed, and at an outlet outside the supermarket at **JQ's Mall**, Rodney Bay. Many fishermen still sell their catch wherever they can. Fish is cheap and fresh.

## Music

**Vibes Music Store**, Rodney Bay Shopping Centre, **T** 4580056, www.vibesmusicstore.com *Map 3, F6, p207* All the latest releases in a variety of styles.

**Vintage Music**, 83 Brazil St, Castries, **T** 4525079. *Map 2, H3, p206*

## Shopping malls

**Gablewoods Shopping Mall**, between Rodney Bay and Castries. *Map 1, C4, p204* Has a selection of boutiques, gift shops, book shop, post office, pharmacy, deli, open-air eating places and **Julian's Supermarket**. Next door is a delicatessen. A few doors away is the **Sea Island Cotton Shop**, the main outlet for Caribelle Batik clothes.

**Pointe Seraphine**, next to the main port in Castries. *Shops open Mon-Fri 0900-1600, Sat 0900-1400. Map 2, D1, p206* Duty-free shopping centre, so take your airline ticket and passport, with many tourist-orientated outlets, restaurants, entertainment and tour operators. Goods bought here can be delivered directly to the airport. Cruise ships can tie up at the complex's own berths.

**La Place Carenage** along Jeremie Street on what used to be called the Northern Wharf on the waterfront. *Map 2, F3, 206 Mon-Fri 0900-1600, Sat 0900-1400.* New shopping centre with duty-free shops: jewellers, internet access, gift shops and craft shops. A smaller version of Pointe Seraphine

**JQ Mall**, Rodney Bay. *Map 3, F5, p207* Also a duty-free facility. On the top floor there is a local arts and crafts outlet guaranteed 100% St Lucian.

---

### Supermarkets

**Glace Supermarket**, Rodney Bay, opposite the marina, **T** 4584595. *Map 1, A5, p204*

**Julian's Supermarket**, Rodney Bay, underneath Cinema 2000 *Mon-Thu 0700-2200, Sat 0700-2400, Sun 0800-1600, holidays 0800-1300, closed Good Friday and Christmas Day.* Also at Gablewoods Shopping Mall *Mon-Thu 0800- 2000, Fri, Sat until 2100, Sun 0800-1300) Map 3, F6, p207*

**JQ's supermarket**, at the traffic lights at the end of the Vigie runway. *Mon-Fri 0800-1900, Sat 0800-1600. Map 1, C4, p204* Fair range of goods, bank next door. Also supermarket on the William Peter Blvd.

**Shopping**

Cricket and football are the main spectator sports. Basketball, netball and volleyball are also popular. Every village has a cricket game at weekends or after work in the season, using makeshift equipment such as sticks or palm frond bases as bats. An Olympic Sports Ground has been built in the south of the island, but is little used as it is so far away from Castries, where most of the athletes and school children live. However, international track and field events as well as football tournaments are held here.

There is some excellent diving and snorkelling off the west coast and you can also fish, sail, windsurf and kitesurf and hire all manner of water toys. On land, there are acres of forest trails for hiking, biking and riding as well as a good golf course and tennis courts at many of the hotels.

### Useful websites and ticket information

For information on cricket in the Caribbean some useful websites include:
www.caribbeancricket.com
www.windiescricket.com
http://uk.cricinfo.com
www.cwcricket.com.

For tickets for international matches, call the windies ticketline, **T** 1-800-744-GAME, toll free in the Caribbean.

## Cricket

**Beausejour Cricket Ground**, **T** 4578834/4578831, *Map 1, A5, p204*  St Lucia hosted its first Test Match in 2003 between the West Indies and Sri Lanka at the Beausejour Cricket Ground and many more Test and international matches have been held here. In 2004 during the England tour of the West Indies, it won the accolade of having the best pitch in the Caribbean and the ground was immaculate. The stands are sponsored by local businesses: *FICS, Air Jamaica, Harry Edwards Jewellers, Bounty Rum* and *Julian's* on the side which gets the morning sun with only a few rows of shade at the top. *JC's* stand gets more shade until later in the day. The Piton mound and the party stand have no shade. For the cricket World Cup in 2007 new stands will be erected. St Lucia is to host the first round matches of the group anchored by England and one semi-final game.

!  There are no St Lucian men in the West Indies cricket team
•  but there are several St Lucian women in the ladies' team.

Sports

## Cycling

**Bike St Lucia**, on a beach just north of Anse Chastanet (linked to *Scuba St Lucia*) **T** 4597755, www.bikestlucia.com  *Map 1, H1, p205* They offer off-road riding on trails through 400 acres of forest (jungle biking). They have a fleet of Cannondale F800 CAAD-3 bikes, which are not for use away from their trails. Accessible only by boat, they organize transfers from your hotel, lunch, snorkelling, etc, US$89.

**Carib Travel**, Micoud St, Castries, **T** 452215.  *Map 2, G4, p206* They have 15 Rockhoppers and offer a trip starting at Paix Bouche through mountain villages down to Gros Islet. Cycling has become popular, mostly in groups with a guide.

**Island Bike Hikes**, Castries, **T** 4580908, www.cyclestlucia.com Vehicle-supported and tailor-made bike tours from US$58, a great way to explore the beaches of the northeast coast.

## Fishing

Fishing trips for barracuda, mackerel, king fish, sailfish, wahoo, dorado, tuna and marlin can be arranged. Several sport fishing boats sail from Rodney Bay Marina.
**Captain Mike's Sportfishing Cruises T** 4527044
**Boating in Paradise T** 4580170
**Hackshaws Boat Charters & Sportfishing T** 4530553
**Mako Water-Sports T** 4520412
**Trivial Pursuit Charters T** 452 5593
For more information, see www.worldwidefishing.com/stlucia

! Recently a 940 lb blue marlin has been landed putting the earlier St Lucian record of 705 lbs in the shade.

Half- and full-day fishing charters cost anywhere between US$380 and US$1000 depending on the size of boat.

There is always the possibility that you will have the pleasure of siting migrating whales and many of the charter companies also do specific whale- and dolphin-watching trips.

## Golf

**St Lucia Golf & Country Club**, Cap Estate, **T** 4508523, www.stluciagolf.com *Map 1, A5, p204* A 6,829-yd, par 71, 18-hole golf course and driving range, green fee US$70 for nine holes, US$95 for 18 holes, golf carts mandatory. Club rental, Pro Shop, restaurant and group packages available.

## Gyms

Many of the larger hotels have gyms for their guests' use.

**Body Inc**, Gablewoods Mall, **T** 4519744. *Map 1, C4, p204* Open daily with state of the art cardio and gym equipment, weights and circuit classes.

**Doolittle's Gym**, Marigot Beach Club, Marigot Bay, **T** 4514974, *0800-2000. Map 1, E3, p204* Gym equipment, weights and aerobics classes.

**Mango Moon Total Fitness**, Vigie Cove, **T** 4531934 *Map 2, C1, p204* Aerobic and fitness classes and well-equipped gym.

**Sportivo Fitness**, Rodney Bay, **T** 4528899. *Map 3, F7, p207* Aerobics, step and fitness classes, well-equipped gym.

## Horse racing

Ask at **Trim's Stables** (see below) for information on horse racing, usually held on public holidays at Cas-en-Bas and in Vieux Fort.

## Horse riding

**Belle Cheval**, Cas-en-Bas, **T** 5191280. *Map 1, A5, p204* US$40 1-hr, US$55 2 hrs, US$75 half-day trip with beach barbecue. They will arrange champagne breakfasts, barbecues and picnics. Prices usually include transfers and service is very good.

**East Coast Riding Stables**, Fond d'Or, **T** 4533242 *Map 1, F7, p204*

**International Pony Club**, Beausejour, Gros Ilet, **T** 4528139, www.stluciatravel.com.lc/internat.htm *Map 1, A5, p204* Trail rides and caters for all levels, choice of English or Western style, US$35 1 hr, US$50 2hrs, US$70 half-day picnic trip.

**North Point Riding Stables**, Cap Estate, **T** 4508853. *Map 1, A5, p204* Takes groups to Cas-en-Bas Beach, Donkey Beach, Pigeon Point or Gros Islet, US$35 1½ hrs, min age 12.

**Trim's Stables**, Cas-en-Bas, **T** 4508273. *Map 1, A5, p204* Riding for beginners or advanced; also offers lessons, 1-hr rides US$40, 2 hrs US$50 and picnic trips to the Atlantic, US$75.

**White Cedar Riding Stables**, Vieux Fort *Map 1, L5, p204*

## Sailing

At Marigot Bay and Rodney Bay you can hire any size of craft, the larger ones coming complete with crew if you want. Many of these yachts sail down to the Grenadines. Rodney Bay has been developed to accommodate 1,000 yachts (with 232 berths in a full-service boatyard and additional moorings in the lagoon) and hosts the annual **Atlantic Rally for Cruisers** race, with about 250 yachts arriving there in December. Charters can be arranged to sail to neighbouring islands. Soufrière has a good anchorage, but as the water is deep it is necessary to anchor close in. There is a pier for short term tie-ups (see also p23).

**Destination St Lucia (DSL)**, Rodney Bay Marina, **T** 4528531. *Map 3, E6, p207* Yachts from 38-52 ft, bareboat charters, multilingual staff.

**The Moorings**, Marigot Bay, **T** 4514357. *Map 1, E3, p204* Bareboat fleet of 38-50 ft Beneteaus and crewed fleet of 50-60 ft yachts, 45-room hotel for accommodation prior to departure or on return, watersports, diving, windsurfing.

## Scuba diving

There is some very good diving off the west coast, although this is somewhat dependent on the weather, as heavy rain tends to create high sediment loads in the rivers and sea. Diving off the east coast is not so good and can be risky unless you are a competent diver. One of the best beach entry dives in the Caribbean is directly off **Anse Chastanet**, where an underwater shelf drops off from about 10 ft down to 60 ft and there is a good dive over **Turtle Reef** in the bay, where there are over 25 different types of **coral**. Below the **Petit Piton** are impressive sponge and coral

**Sports**

communities on a drop to 200 ft of spectacular wall. There are gorgonians, black coral trees, huge barrel sponges and plenty of other beautiful reef life. **Dive sites**, running north to south, are Turtle Reef, Anse Chastanet Reef, Fairyland, Grand Caille, Trou Diable, Pinnacles (an impressive site where four pinnacles rise to within 10 ft of the surface), Hummingbird Wall, Malgretoute, Superman's Flight, Piton Wall, Jalousie, Coral Gardens and The Blue Hole. The area in front of the Anse Chastanet Hotel is a buoyed off **Marine Reserve**, stretching from the west point at Grand Caille North to Chamin Cove. Only the hotel boats and local fishermen's canoes are allowed in. By the jetty, a roped-off area is used by snorkellers and beginner divers. Other popular dive sites include Anse L'Ivrogne, Anse La Raye Point (good snorkelling also at Anse La Raye) and the **wrecks**, such as the *Volga* (in 20 ft of water north of Castries harbour, well broken up, subject to swell, requires caution), the *Waiwinette* (several miles south of Vieux Fort, strong currents, competent divers only), and the 165-ft *Lesleen M* (deliberately sunk in 1986 off Anse Cochon Bay in 60 ft of water).

The Fisheries Department is pursuing an active **marine protection programme**. It is illegal take any coral or undersized shellfish. Corals and sponges should not even be touched. It is also illegal to buy or sell coral products on St Lucia. The Soufrière Marine Management Association, **T** 4595500, www.smma.org.lc, preserves the environment between Anse Chastanet and Anse L'Ivrogne to the south. They have placed moorings in the reserve, which yachts are required to take, charges are on a sliding scale depending on the size of the boat. Collection of marine mammals (dead or alive) is prohibited, spearguns are illegal and anchoring is prohibited. Rangers come by at night to collect the fee and explain the programme, **T** 4522595. Dive moorings have been installed and are being financed with Marine Reserve Fees, US$5 daily, US$15 a year.

● *Visitors must dive with a local company.*

A single-tank dive costs around US$35-55, introductory resort courses are about US$65-90, a six-dive package US$175-200 and open water certification courses US$380-495, plus 10% service charge.

**Aquabulle**, operated by Water Sport World at Rodney Bay Marina, **T** 4584292, watersports@candw.lc. *Map 3, F5, p207* You can see the underwater world without getting wet by taking a ride on this semi-submersible. Departures are at 0900 and 1500, 1½ hrs, US$30 adults, US$15 under 16, one child under 10 free if accompanied by two adults.

**Buddies Scuba**, Rodney Bay Marina, **T/F** 4529086. *Map 3, E6, p207* PADI, BSAC, two-tank day dives, one-tank night dives, camera rental, open water certification or resort course, dive packages available.

**Dive Fair Helen**, Castries, **T** 4517716, www.divefairhelen.com. *Map 2, D1, p206* One dive US$60, two- dive package US$84, PADI Open Water Course US$489, two- dive boats with washroom and shower and shade as well as platform and easy access to the water. Snorkelling and kayaking also offered.

**Frog's Diving**, at Harmony Suites, **T** 4508831, tee-j@candw.lc *Map 3, F5, p207*. PADI courses for all levels. A two-tank dive costs US$90 including all equipment, night diving US$75, Open Water course US$430.

**Island Divers**, Anse Cochon at Ti Kaye hotel. *Map 1, F2, p204* Run by Terroll and his team. A beginner's resort course costs US$75, a two-tank dive is US$70 including tank, weights, mask, fins and snorkel, other equipment for rent.

Sports

**Moorings Scuba Centre**, Marigot Bay, **T** 4514357. *Map 1, E3, p204* PADI courses.

**Scuba St Lucia**, Anse Chastanet, www.scubastlucia.com or contact them through the hotel. *Map 1, H2, p205* PADI five-star, SSI and DAN, three dive boats with oxygen on each, photographic hire and film processing, video filming and courses, day and night dives, resort courses and full PADI certification, multilingual staff, pick-up service Monday to Saturday from hotels north of Castries, day packages for divers, snorkellers, beginners and others include lunch and equipment.

### Squash and tennis

Many hotels have tennis courts, some of them lit for night play. There is a squash court near Cap Estate Golf Club House and at the **St Lucia Yacht Club**, **T** 4528350. **The St Lucian Hotel** has two tennis courts for public bookings and lessons, **T** 4528351.

**The St Lucia Racquet Club**, Cap Estate, **T** 4500551. *Map 1, A5, p204* Nine floodlit tennis courts and squash court with instruction. They host an annual competition open to all amateur tennis and squash players.

### Windsurfing and kiteboarding

The winds off **Anse de Sables** in the southeast of the island are very good for both windsurfing and kiteboarding, with the latter taking place off a cove slightly to the north. January, February, May and June are the best months with lots of wind blowing unobstructed cross-onshore from the left. The sickle-shaped beach is bordered leeward by Moule à Chique peninsula, so you are safe from drifting off into the Atlantic. In the summer the wind is unreliable and the operators close until the end of October.

See www.kiteboardingmag.com for an article on St Lucia, also www.stlucia.com/windsurf and www.stluciakiteboarding.com.

**Club Mistral Windsurfing Centre and Sky-riders Kite-surfing Centre**, The Reef Beach Café, Anse de Sables, **T** 4543418. *Map 1, L6, p205*

**Tornado**, Anse de Sables, **T** 4860545, www.tornado-surf.com *Map 1, L6, p205* Run by Elena Sparta, from Italy. Windsurfing with JP boards, Neil Pryde sails, rental prices quoted in Euros but around US$60 a day if booked in advance, weekly rates are cheaper. Courses from introductory and beginner (US$128 for 6 hrs). Kitesurfing with Cabrinha kite and boards, around US$60 a day. An IKO centre with courses for all levels, taster US$204 for 6 hrs including gear, beginner US$312 for 10 hrs. Kite Beach is 100 m leeward side of Tornado. Storage service for your own gear.

St Lucia is every kid's dream, with safe Caribbean beaches to play on and plenty to do inland, exploring the rainforest and finding the birds and animals that inhabit the island, or touring a plantation and learning about the colonial way of life, slavery, pirates and Brigands. Nowhere is far away so they won't get bored in a car for long, although a supply of travel sickness remedies might be useful for the mountain roads. The lack of museums and buildings of architectural interest means you won't be trailing them around in the heat against their will. The beaches are the main attraction, with lots of watersports on offer for kids of all ages, as well as catamaran trips along the coast to avoid the twisty roads. Many families opt for the all-inclusive resorts to entertain their children, but there are plenty of other ways of providing them with stimulation and enjoyment without confining them to the grounds of one hotel. Teenagers will enjoy Friday nights at the Anse La Raye fish fry or the Gros Islet jump-up where there is music and dancing until you or they drop.

> ### ▶ Kid's stuff
>
> Some general tips: the water is drinkable, so there are no worries there and generally if you keep them hydrated and avoid sunburn, you won't have any health problems at all. Avoid the sun between 1100-1500 and take extra care if they are out on a boat, even when the sun isn't shining as the wind and the reflection can burn badly. Always carry bottled water with you.

## Eating and drinking

Kids are accepted at most hotels, although some of the *Sandals* properties are for couples only. At the smaller hotels they are welcomed and many now have self-catering facilities so you can prepare snacks and light meals when they are needed. Food is easy, with lots of places selling burgers, pizzas, pasta or chicken and chips. Most restaurants have international-style menus with local specialities to tempt the adventurous. Life is a little easier if they eat fish.

## Sights

**Forestière Rainforest Trail**, Forestry Department, Forestière, **T** 4516168, forestrails@slumaffe.org  *20 mins' drive from Castries. Bus 5E from Castries.  Guides available Mon-Fri, 0830-1500. Pay on site, US$10.   Map 1, D5, p204  See also p44*

This three-mile, two-hour trail is a good activity in the shade if the kids have had enough sun on the beach but still want to be out of doors. It is an easy trail but with enough steps, ups and downs for it to feel like a jungle adventure for children. Make sure they wear trainers or good shoes; it can be muddy and slippery in places.

Tour operators bring parties here in the mornings, so come in the afternoon for a quieter time, but not too late otherwise the guides go home. It is a good introduction to the rainforest and the guide will point out incense trees oozing white sap with a pungent smell. The chataignier tree has  enormous buttresses which children can climb in.

**Union Agricultural Station**, Forestry Department, **T** 4502231 Ext 316, www.geocities.com/sluforestrails  *Where the John Compton Highway leaves Choc Bay and just before it crosses the Choc River, a right turn to Babonneau will take you past the Union Agricultural station (about one mile).*  Map 1, C5, p204  See also p46 Union is the site of the Forestry Department headquarters, where there is a visitor centre, nature trail and the nearest thing St Lucia gets to a zoo. Here, children can see indigenous species such as the agouti and the boa constrictor and the endemic St Lucia parrot as well as species which have been introduced. There is a hillside trail, a one-mile loop through tropical dry forest, with some steps and rough ground but an easy walk at a leisurely pace which should take no more than a couple of hours.

**Pigeon Island**  *About ¾ mile after Elliot's Shell filling station on the outskirts of Gros Islet, turn left.  Daily 0900-1700; museum closed Sun. Entry to park and museum EC$10 visitors, EC$5 residents (free after 1700 but only to the restaurants).*  Map 3, B3/4, p207  See also p49 Fortresses, naval battles against the French, pirates and Brigands have all left their mark on Pigeon Island and it is a great place for children to explore military ruins and enjoy the view of Rodney Bay. Once an island, Pigeon Island is now joined to the mainland by a causeway. It has two peaks which are joined by a saddle. On the lower of the two peaks lies Fort Rodney, which you can climb up to. Amerindian remains have been found, the French pirate François Leclerc (known as 'Jambe de Bois' for his wooden leg) used the large cave on the north shore and the Duke of Montagu tried to colonize it in 1722 (but abandoned it after one afternoon). From here, Admiral Rodney set sail in 1782 to meet the French navy at the Battle of Les Saintes. It was captured by the Brigands (French slaves freed by the leaders of the French revolution) in 1795 but retaken in 1798 by the British and used as a US observation post during the Second World War. There are a couple of restaurants where you can get full meals, snacks, drinks and ice creams and two small beaches where you can cool off, with plenty of shade under the trees, so you can make a day of it.

**Grande Anse**  Contact Heritage Tours, **T** 4516058, heritagetours@candw.lc  *Map 1, C7, p204  See also p53*
Grande Anse, on the east coast, is a long windy beach, currently not open to the general public although turtle watching is organized from March to July.  This is one of the most important nesting sites in the Caribbean for the leatherback turtle and a great experience for children and adults to see the huge creatures clambering up the sand, digging holes and laying their eggs, completely oblivious of their audience. Visits to Grand Anse to see the turtles can only be done in organized groups on an overnight vigil. You set off at 1600, return around 0700 and will need to take food, drink, a torch, insect repellent, good walking shoes and warm clothing; tents are supplied.  Be prepared for all weathers:  wind, rain or perfect nights.

**Barre de l'Isle Rainforest Trail**, Forestry Department, Union, **T** 4502231, Ext 316, forestrails@slumaffe.org  *30 mins' drive from Castries. Access from the main road, parking by a snack bar where the guides wait. Bus 2B or 2C from Castries.  Guides available Mon-Fri, 0830-1500. Pay on site, US$10. Guides can be arranged at weekends but will cost more.  Map 1, F5, p204  See also p56*
If you are driving across the island, this is a convenient place to stop and stretch your legs as a break from the winding mountain roads. There is a short, circular trail at the high point on the road

Kids

between Castries and Dennery, which takes about 10 minutes and affords good views of the rainforest and down the Roseau valley. There is a small picnic shelter and toilet at 800 ft with a view down to the Caribbean. A boa constrictor can often be found sleeping in a tree nearby. Alternatively, for a longer walk the main trail is about a mile long and takes an hour, coming back on the same path. There are several lookout points from where you can see Morne Gimie, the Cul-de-Sac valley on the west and the Mabouya valley and Fond d'Or on the east. On the trail you might just glimpse the colourful St Lucia parrot among many other birds while mongoose and agouti also live in the forest.

**Maria Islands**, The National Trust, head office, **T** 4525005, Southern Regional office **T** 4545014, natrust@candw.lc
*US$35/EC$94 per person for two people for boat and guide. By reservation only. Unauthorized access is not allowed. Package of transport, tour, lunch for min 4 people is US$75 per person.*
*Map 1, F5, p204  See also p67*  This trip is well worth doing as you get a combination of nature tour, boat ride and beach, all in a spectacular setting with tremendous views over St Lucia. The Maria Islands, just offshore, are home to two endemic reptiles, a colourful lizard and small, very rare, harmless grass snake, the St Lucia racer, also known as the *kouwès* or couresse snake. The lizard is known as *zandoli tè* in Kwéyòl and lives only here and on Praslin Island, where it was introduced to protect numbers. The males, about 18 cm long, sport the colours of the national flag. The females are brown with some white spots along their belly. You will hear them scuttling under bushes so keep your ears and eyes peeled. There are several other lizards on the island, including the rock gecko which hides in cracks in the rocks. The couresse snake can often be found in the hollow of a forked tree where a pool of water has collected as it likes to keep damp and cool. The guide will point it out to you if it is at home as well as all the other creatures. You will be given life jackets for the crossing. Take trainers or walking shoes

as flip flops are unsatisfactory for the rocky parts of the trail and there are cactus spines. Be prepared to get wet getting into the boat as there is no jetty, but the boat men will help you and carry small children. There is a nice beach on the leeward side of Maria Major facing back to Anse de Sables and the snorkelling is good, so take your mask and fins. If you go on a tour with an agency they will provide gear but the National Trust does not. When you get back to the mainland, Anse de Sables is a long sweep of sandy beach, which is safe for swimming, and there are beach bars. Take plenty of sun screen.

**Eastern Caribbean Butterfly House**, Lovers Lane, **T** 4597429, stluciabutterflyhouse@yahoo.com *4 blocks from the RC church, just off Sir Arthur Lewis St. Daily 1000-1700. US$6/EC$16. Map 1, I2, p205 See also p78* If you are touring the west coast with the aim of visiting the Sulphur Springs, children might like to stop off in Soufrière to see the Butterfly House, the only one in the Windwards. Imported pupae from Central America and the Caribbean are hatched and grown in a small house then set loose. Over 60 colourful varieties are flying around freely in the tropical garden setting.

**Sulphur Springs** *Take the Vieux Fort road between wooden houses about halfway along the south side of Soufrière square. Follow the road for about two miles and you will see a sign on the left. You will smell the springs before you reach them. Daily 0900-1700. EC$3. Tour with guide takes about 30 mins. Map 1, I3, p205 See also p80* There are not many opportunities in the world to see an active volcano, but this is one of them and a great experience for kids, where they can smell the fumes and feel the heat. Originally a huge volcano about 3 miles in diameter, it collapsed some 40,000 years ago leaving the west part of the rim empty (where you drive in). The sign welcomes you to the world's only drive-in volcano, although actually you have to stop at a car park. The sulphur spring is the only one still active, although there are seven cones within the old crater as well as the Pitons which are thought to be volcanic plugs. Tradition has it that the Arawak god *Yokahu* slept here and it was therefore the site of human sacrifices. The Caribs were less superstitious but still named it *Qualibou,* the place of death. From the main viewing platform, you can see over a moonscape of bubbling, mineral rich, grey mud pools. One of these pools, known as *Gabriel's hole*, was created when a guide jumped around too much. He received second-degree burns from the waist down, but survived after medical attention in Martinique and now works as a fisherman. The hole is still growing and no one is now allowed near the pools, with visitors confined to the viewing platform. Your guide will explain everything and answer all the questions you can think to ask.

# Directory

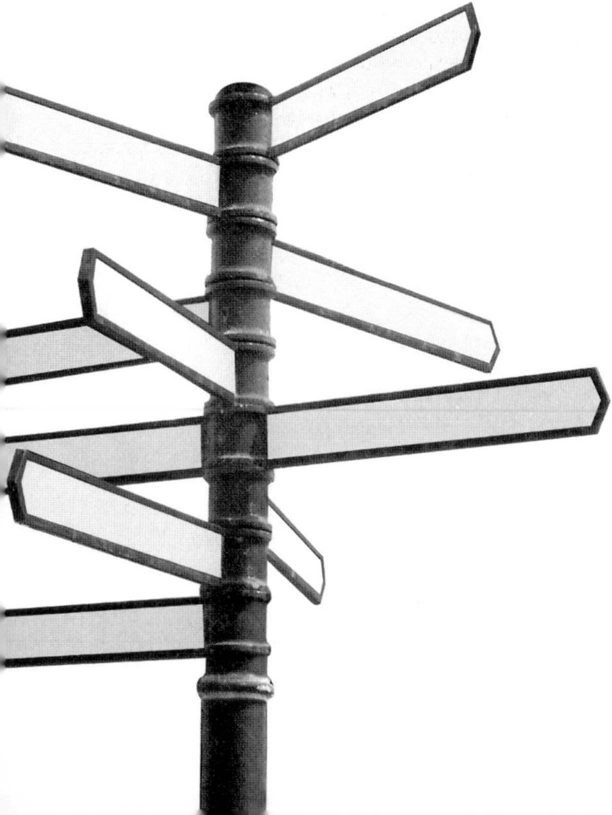

## Airline offices

**Air Canada**, Bridge St, Castries, **T** 4523051, Hewanorra **T** 4546249, Toll free **T** 1-800-7442472. **Air Caraïbes**, George F L Charles Airport, **T** 4530357. **Air Jamaica**, Hewanorra Airport, **T** 4548870, Reservations, **T** 1-800-5235585. **American Eagle**, George F L Charles Airport, **T** 4521820/1840. **British Airways**, 15-17 Brazil St, Clico Building, Castries, **T** 4527444/3951, Hewanorra Airport, **T** 4546172. **BWIA**, Micoud St, Castries, **T** 1-800-5382942, Hewanorra Airport, **T** 4545075. **Caribbean Star**, 20 Bridge St, Castries, **T** 4532927, Toll free **T** 1-800-744star. **LIAT**, Brazil St, Castries, **T** 4523051, George F L Charles Airport, **T** 188-8445428. **St Lucia Helicopters**, Island Flyers Hangar, George F L Charles Airport, **T** 4536950. **Virgin Atlantic**, Hewanorra Airport, **T** 4543610, Toll free **T** 1-800-7447477.

## Banks and ATMs

Banks' opening hours vary, but most are open *Mon-Thu 0800-1500 Fri 0800-1700*, FirstCaribbean International, Bank of Nova Scotia, St Lucia Co-operative Bank and Royal Bank of Canada at Rodney Bay *open Sat until 1200*. Nearly all banks have ATMs.

**Bank of Nova Scotia**, William Peter Blvd, Castries, **T** 4562100, Corner High St and Chaussee Rd, **T** 4523797, Rodney Bay, **T** 4528805, Vieux Fort, **T** 4546314. **Bank of St Lucia**, Bridge St, Castries, **T** 4566000, Vieux Fort, **T** 4547780, Gros Islet, **T** 4500928, Soufrière, **T** 4597450. **FirstCaribbean International Bank**, William Peter Blvd, Castries, **T** 4523751, Bridge St, **T** 4561000, Rodney Bay Marina, **T** 4529384, Vieux Fort **T** 4546255, Soufrière, **T** 4597255. **RBTT Bank**, Micoud St, Castries, **T** 4517469, Gablewoods Mall, **T** 4522265. **Royal Bank of Canada**, William Peter Blvd, **T** 4569200, Rodney Bay, **T** 4529921. **St Lucia Co-Operative Bank**, Bridge St, Castries, **T** 4557000, JQ Mall, Rodney Bay, **T** 4528882, Vieux Fort, **T** 4546213.

## Bicycle hire
**Bike St Lucia**, **T** 4597755, www.bikestlucia.com
**Carib Travel**, **T** 4522151  **Island Bike Hikes**, **T** 4580908,
www.cyclestlucia.com  *See also Cycling tours, p30 and Cycling p154*

## Car hire
**Alto Rent-A-Car**, Castries, **T** 4520233, Hewanorra, **T** 4545311.
**Avis**, Hewanorra, **T** 4546325, George F L Charles Airport,
**T** 4522046, Pointe Seraphine, **T** 4522700, and lots of other
locations. Reservations **T** 4516976. **Budget**, **T** 4529887,
Hewanorra, **T** 4547470, www.budgetstlucia.net  **Candida**, Rodney
Bay, **T** 4527076.**Cool Breeze Jeep Rental**, Soufrière, **T** 4597729,
Castries, **T** 4582031. **Courtesy**, Bay Gardens Inn, **T** 4528140.
**Hertz**, headquarters at Rodney Bay, **T** 4520680, Hewanorra,
**T** 4549636, George F L Charles, **T** 4517351. **National**, Massade,
Gros Islet Highway, **T** 4508721, also at Lobster Pot, Beanfield, Vieux
Fort, **T** 4546699, and at Pointe Seraphine, **T** 4530085,
carrental@candw.lc  **TJ's**, Rodney Bay, **T** 4520116.

## Consulates
*(also see under Embassies)*
**Denmark and Sweden**, **T** 4500190, royalknight@candw.lc
*Mon-Fri 1000-1200*.  **Dominican Republic**, corner Brazil and
Mongiraud streets, **T** 4527865, F 4522931.  *Mon-Fri 0830-1200,
1330-1700*. **Germany**, Gros Islet, **T** 45080500, karencave@candw.lc
**Guyana**, American Drywall Building, Castries, **T** 4530309  *Mon-Fri
0800-1630*.  **Jamaica**, 27 Micoud St, Castries, **T** 4523040  *Mon-Fri
0800-1630*.  **Italy**, Reduit, **T** 4520865, spicetravel@casalucia.com
**Netherlands**, M & C Building, Bridge St, Castries, **T** 4523592,
peterd.mc@candw.lc  *Mon-Fri 0800-1630*.  **Norway**, Ward &
Company Building, Bridge St, Castries, **T** 4522216.  *Mon-Fri
0800-1630*.

## Credit card lines

**American Express**, **T** 1-800-3271267.
**Mastercard**, **T** 1-800-8472911. **Visa**, **T** 1-800-3077309.
For other credit cards without a local or regional contact number,
make sure you bring details from home for a number to call if your
card is lost or stolen.

## Cultural institutions

**Alliance Française de Sainte Lucie**, The Pyramid, Pointe
Seraphine, **T** 452468. *Closed weekends and French public holidays.*

## Dentists

**Dr Kent Glace**, Rodney Bay, **T** 4580167, also has a surgery on
Micoud St, Castries, **T** 4523840 **Dr Worral**, on the highway
opposite LUCELEC and the Vigie Sports Complex, **T** 4524466

## Disabled

A few of the larger hotels have a room or two adapted for
wheelchair users, but generally facilities are limited. Pavements
and sidewalks can be narrow and intermittent, while shops and
restaurants are often reached via steps.

## Doctors

A range of specialists have their offices at Tapion Hospital,
**T** 4592000. For emergencies go to the Gros Islet PolyClinic.
**Gail Devaux-Segovia** and **Carlos Segovia** are naturopaths
with a clinic behind the Rainbow Hotel, Rodney Bay, **T** 4528176,
www.gocaribbeanblue.com, and a range of natural products.

## Electricity

Voltage 220 v, 50 cycles. A few hotels are 110 v, 60 cycles. Most
sockets take three-pin square plugs (UK standard), but some take
two-pin round plugs or flat US plugs. Adaptors generally available
in hotels.

## Embassies
**British High Commission**, NIS Building, Waterfront, Castries, **T** 4522484, **F** 4531543  *Mon-Thu 0800-1600, Fri 0800-1300.*
**Cuba**, Rodney Heights, **T** 4584665, embacubasantalucia@candw.lc *Mon-Fri 0930-1400.*  **France**, Vigie Rd, **T** 4556060, **F** 4556056, *Mon-Tue, Thu-Fri 0800-1500, Wed 0830-1300.*  **Venezuela**, Casa Vigie, **T** 4524033, vembassy@candw.lc  *Mon-Fri 0800-1500.*

## Emergency numbers
**T** 911.
**Aerojet Ambulance**, **T** 4521600, **F** 4532229. For air evacuation.

## Hospitals
**Victoria Hospital**, Castries, **T** 4522421/4537059. **St Jude's**, Vieux Fort, **T** 4546041. **Soufrière Casualty**, **T** 4597258. **Dennery**, **T** 4533310. **Tapion**, **T** 4592000. **Gros Islet Polyclinic**, on the main road on the right as you head north, just past the Gros Islet Cas-en-Bas junction, **T** 4509661.  *Mon-Fri 0800-1630.*  Very efficient, good patient care, inexpensive, eg a course of tetanus shots is US$10. **The Rodney Bay Medical Centre**, **T** 4528621, is a collection of private doctors and dentists on the left just inside the turning to JQ's Mall. Larger hotels have resident doctors or doctors 'on call', visits cost about EC$50. If given a prescription, ask at the Pharmacy whether the medication is available 'over the counter', as this may be cheaper.

## Gay and Lesbian
Homosexuality is illegal in St Lucia and the island is one of the more backward in the Caribbean in its approach to gay visitors. Some of the larger resort hotels still specify heterosexual couples only. Others are more tolerant but as a general rule stick to the smaller hotels and guesthouses.

### Internet/email

Services at the **Gablewoods Mall** office of **Cable & Wireless**, EC$5 for 30 minutes, at **Jambe de Bois** on Pigeon Island, EC$10 per hour, and also in the **University Centre**. **ClickCom**, Shop 9, La Place Carenage, **T** 4524444, clickcom@candw.lc has broadband at US$12 per hour, phones and prepaid cards, bank CDs and floppy disks and cameras. Many hotels offer internet services to guests.

### Library

There are small libraries in most towns and most are open every morning (*Mon-Sat, 1000-1300*) and sometimes to 1800 on certain days. **Castries Central Library**, Bourbon Street at the corner of Micoud Street, Castrires**T** 4522875, clibrary@isis.org.lc  The neo-classical library on the west side of Derek Walcott Square is the largest active lending library on the island with sections on fiction and children's books, but it is also used for evening lectures and talks.

### Media

**Newspapers**  St Lucia's main titles are the *Voice* out on Tue Thu and Sat; the *Mirror* on Fri and the *Star* on Mon, Wed and Fri. *One Caribbean* is a weekend paper out on Sat and the *Crusader* is a free paper with local events also out on Sat.

**Radio**  The commercial radio station, **Radio Caribbean International** (RCI), broadcasts daily in Kwéyòl and English, and the government-owned station, **Radio St Lucia** (RSL), broadcasts in Kwéyòl and English. It has some fine programmes such as Sports Zone and if you want to hear the concerns of St Lucians listen to Constitution Park at 1400 (only the Thursday broadcast is in Kwéyòl). RCI and RSL have two FM and an AM station each. Other stations are **Radio 100** (Helen FM); the **Wave** (formerly GEM) has two FM, and broadcasts rhythm and soul.

**Television**  Local stations: Government station NTV on Channel 3, HTS on Channel 4 and DBS on Channel 10. HTS has an occasional programme in Kwéyòl and speeches by government officials. There is much cable TV. On cable (in hotels), NTN National Television Network is on 2, Helen TV is on 34 and DBS on 35.

## Motorcycle hire
**Wayne's Motorcycle Centre**, Vide Bouteille, **T** 4520680.   Rents bikes; make sure you wear a helmet and have adequate insurance.

## Pharmacies
**Clarke's Drug Store**, Bridge St, Castries, **T** 4522727. **Fitz St Rose Medical Centre**, Micoud St, Castries, **T** 4520785. **HUS Pharmacy**, Boid d'Orange, **T** 4528271. **M&C Drug Store**, Bridge St, Castries, **T** 4522811, at Gablewoods Mall, **T** 4588151, JQ's Mall, Rodney Bay, **T** 4588153, JQ's Plaza, Vieux Fort, **T** 4588154, Julian's at Rodney Bay. **Williams Pharmacy**, Bridge St, Castries, **T** 4522797.

## Police
**Police Headquarters**, Bridge St, Castries, **T** 4522854. **Police Rapid Response Unit**, **T** 4522854 Ext 167. Any crimes should be reported to your hotel, the Tourist Board and/or the police.

## Post offices
**Main post office** is on Bridge St, Castries, *open Mon-Fri, 0830-1630, Sat 0800-1200*, poste restante at the rear. Other branches in Gablewoods and JQ's Malls. Postcards to Europe EC$0.75, to the USA, UK and Canada EC$0.65, unsealed cards EC$0.50; letters to Europe EC$1.10, to the USA, Canada and UK EC$0.95.
**DHL Worldwide Express**, 20 Bridge St, Castries, **T** 4531538. **Federal Express**, Castries, **T** 4521320. **LIAT Quick Pak**, 20 Bridge St, Castries, **T** 4560455. **Parcels Express**, Vide Bouteille, **T** 4527211. **UPS**, Castries, **T** 4525898. **Erands Courier Services**, Cadet St, Castries, **T** 4526709, erands911@hotmail.com

## Public holidays

**New Year's Day** (1 and 2 January)  **Independence Day** (22 February)  **Good Friday  Easter Monday  Labour Day** (1 May)  **Whit Monday  Corpus Christi  Carnival  Emancipation Day** (1 August)  **Thanksgiving Day** (first Monday in October)  **National Day** (13 December)  **Christmas Day** (25 December)  **Boxing Day** (26 December)

## Religious services

Most St Lucians are Roman Catholic but there are also Anglican churches, Methodist, Baptist, Seventh Day Adventist, Pentecostal, Christian Science and other denominations. Services are held Sunday mornings and in the larger churches there are Sunday evening services as well.

## Taxi firms

Fares are set by the Government, but the US$60 Castries-Soufrière fare doubles as unlucky tourists discover that there are no buses for the return journey. Club St Lucia, in the extreme north, to Castries, about 10 miles away, costs US$15-18 one way for one-four people, US$3.75 per additional passenger. Fare from Castries to Gros Islet (for Friday evening street party), US$12; to Pigeon Island National Park, US$15.50 one way; to Vigie Airport, US$5; to Hewanorra Airport, US$56; Vigie Airport to Rodney Bay US$16; Marigot Bay to Hewanorra Airport US$45; to Vigie Airport US$22, to Castries US$20 (30 minutes). If in doubt about the amount charged, check with the tourist office or hotel reception. You can see a copy of the fixed fares at the airport. At rush hour it is almost impossible to get a taxi so allow plenty of time, the traffic jams are amazing for such a small place. A trip round the island by taxi is about US$20 per hour for one-four people, with an additional US$5 per hour for air conditioning.

Recommended taxi drivers are Kenneth James, **T** 4536844/4519778, Barnard Henry, **T** 4501951, Samson Louis, **T** 4500516 (or through the Rex St Lucian taxi stand) and Raymond Cepal, pager **T** 4843583. There are also **Courtesy Taxi Service**, Jeremie and Coral streets, **T** 4523555, **George FL Charles Airport Taxi Service**, **T** 4521599, **Southern Taxi**, Hewanorra Airport, **T** 4546136 and **Vieux Fort Taxi Service**, **T** 4542643, among others.

## Telephone
**Cable and Wireless**, no longer has a monopoly and has been joined by **Digicel** and **AT&T**, www.attwireless.com/caribbean, all with offices on Bridge St, Castries. Hotels do not generally allow direct dialling, you will have to go through the operator, which can be slow and costly. Charges vary, depending on time of day and day of week. Pay phones use EC$0.25 and EC$1 coins or cards. Cable and Wireless phone cards are sold for EC$10, EC$20, EC$40 or EC$50 plus tax (a EC$10 card costs EC$11); with these you can phone abroad.

There is a credit card phone at Vigie Airport operated via the boat phone network, open daily 0800-2200. Call **USA T** 1-800-6747000; **Sprint Express T** 1-800-2777468; **BT Direct T** 1-800-3425284; **Canada Direct T** 1-800-7442580; **USA Direct** phone at Rodney Bay Marina, or **T** 1-800-8722881. If you want to dial a toll-free US number, replace the 800 with 400. You will be charged a local call.

## Time
Atlantic Standard Time, 1 hr ahead of EST, 4 hrs behind GMT (5 hrs behind Europe in summer time).

## Toilets
Public toilets are few and far between, but in Soufrière there are some behind the Shell garage, turn left as you come over the bridge into town from the north, by the traffic lights.

## Travel agents

**Barnards Travel Agency**, Bridge St, Castries, **T** 4522214.
**Carib Travel Agency**, Micoud St, Castries, **T** 4522151.
**Hibiscus Travel Agency**, Bourbon St, Castries, T 4531527.
**International Travel Consultants**, Bourbon St, Castries,
**T** 4523131. *L'Express Des Isles*, **Cox & Co**, William Peter Blvd,
Castries, **T** 4522211. **Pitons Travel Agency**, Richard Fanis Building,
Marisule, Gros Islet, T 4501486. **Travel World**, American Drywall
Building, Vide Bouteille Highway, Castries, **T** 4517443,
travelworld@candw.lc **Solar Tours & Travel**, Castries, T 4525898.
**St Lucia Reps/Sunlink Tours**, **T** 4528232, www.stluciareps.com
**Spice Travel**,**T** 4520866, www.casalucia.com **Barefoot Holidays**,
**T** 4500507, www.travelfile.com/get/baredays.html

# A sprint through history

**1502**  It is believed that Christopher Columbus sailed past the island but missed it completely.

**1520**  A Vatican globe marked the island as Santa Lucía, suggesting that it was claimed by Spain.

**1605**  The first European attempts to settle the island of *Iouanalao*, or *Hewanorra*, were repulsed by the Caribs, who were living on the island having overpowered the Arawaks, who had moved up the island chain before them. There is evidence of a Dutch expedition and also the arrival of 67 Englishmen en route to Guiana.

**1638**  The first recorded settlement was made by English from Bermuda and St Kitts but the colonists were killed by the Caribs about three years later.

**1642**  The King of France, claiming sovereignty over the island, ceded it to the *French West India Company*.

**1650**  The *French West India Company* sold the island to M Houel and M Du Parquet. There were several attempts by the Caribs to expel the French and several governors were murdered.

**1660**  The British began to renew their claim to the island and fighting for possession began in earnest. The settlers were mostly French, who developed a plantation economy based on slave labour.

**1762**  British forces under Admiral George Rodney took St Lucia, only to lose it again in 1763.

**1778**  War erupted again. Admiral Rodney wrote that St Lucia was a far greater prize than neighbouring

Martinique because of its excellent harbour, then called Carénage (now Castries).

| 1782 | Admiral Rodney led the English fleet in an epic assault on the French navy, on its way to attack Jamaica. The Battle of Les Saintes took place around the French islands of Les Saintes and resulted in the death of some 14,000 French soldiers and sailors when Rodney broke the French formation, allowing his ships to encircle and fire broadsides into the helpless French vessels. The battle marked a turning point in the political balance of power and recognized British supremacy in the West Indies. However, in the subsequent *Treaty of Versailles*, St Lucia was returned to France and fighting continued intermittently. |

| 1796 | During the French Revolution, Victor Hugues, used his base in St Lucia to support insurrections in nearby islands. The guillotine was erected in Castries and the island became known by the French as St Lucie La Fidèle. Britain invaded again and fought a protracted campaign against a guerrilla force of white and black republicans known as *L'Armée Française dans les bois*, until it was finally pacified by General John Moore. |

| 1814 | The *Treaty of Paris* awarded St Lucia to Britain and it became a British Crown Colony, having changed hands 14 times. |

| 1834 | Britain abolished slavery. |

Background

| 1838 | The island was included in a Windward Islands Government, with a Governor resident first in Barbados and then in Grenada. |
|------|------|
| 1885 | St Lucia was chosen as one of Britain's two main coaling stations, selling Welsh coal to passing steam ships. |
| 1897 | 947 ships entered Castries harbour, 620 of them steam powered, and Castries was the fourteenth most important port in the world in terms of tonnage handled. |
| 1935 | The rise of oil brought the decline of coal. When coal workers went on strike, the Governor brought in a warship and marines patrolled the streets in a show of strength. No wage rises were granted. |
| 1937 | Sugar workers went on strike for higher wages. A small increase in wages was agreed. |
| 1939 | St Lucia's first trade union was formed, which grew into the St Lucia Labour Party (SLP), led by George FL Charles (1916-2004). |
| 1951 | Universal adult suffrage was introduced. The SLP won the elections and retained power until 1964. George Charles was the first Chief Minister. He pushed through several constitutional reforms, enhancing labour legislation for the benefit of workers and introducing the system of ministerial government. The sugar industry declined and bananas were promoted as suitable for smallholder production, eventually dominating the island's economy. |

| 1958 | St Lucia joined the short-lived West Indies Federation. |
|------|----------|
| 1964 | The United Workers' Party (UWP) won the elections, led by Mr John Compton. He held power in 1964-79 and subsequently won elections in 1982, 1987 and 1992. |
| 1967 | St Lucia gained full internal self-government, becoming a State in voluntary association with Great Britain. The first St Lucian Governor General was appointed, Sir Frederick Clarke (1912-80), serving from 1967-71. |
| 1979 | St Lucia gained full independence. |
| 1996 | Mr Compton retired as leader of the UWP and was replaced as Prime Minister and leader of the party by Dr Vaughan Lewis. |
| 1997 | The SLP triumphed in the elections, winning 16 of the 17 seats in the Assembly, and Dr Kenny Anthony became Prime Minister. |
| 2001 | The SLP was returned with a smaller majority, winning 14 seats. Its popularity had slipped in areas hit by the banana crisis and the world economic downturn with its knock-on effects on the tourism industry. |
| 2004 | When Sir George Charles, pioneer of the labour movement and the island's first Chief Minister, died on 26 June 2004, his body was put on view on the market steps at his own request. |

# Art and architecture

**18th century**

St Lucia's architecture carries strong French influences from the days when it was part of the French empire. The old stone plantation houses were destroyed by Brigands at the end of the 18th century and not many timber buildings have survived the hurricanes and fires since then. It was traditional to build in wood, as timber was plentiful, but there were drawbacks. In 1785 the Baron de Laborie wrote "The hurricane of 1780 destroyed all the churches, except that of Dauphin, and it is still the only one in existence in the colony." Good examples of French colonial architecture can be found on **Brazil Street** in Castries, and although many buildings have been renovated, they have kept elements of the traditional style.

**19th century**

Most of the old buildings in Castries that were not destroyed by the fire of 1948 date from the 19th and early 20th centuries when the British were the colonial rulers. Nevertheless, the French style dominates. Pretty balconies and verandas framed with intricate latticework form the basis of gingerbread houses. **The Pink House**, on Brogile Street, is a three-storey house built as a family home with shops on the ground floor. The timber wrap-around balcony on the first floor is an example of the traditional latticework. Wooden shutters and jalousie windows were typically used as protection against hurricanes and these can be seen at the Desir family home on Riverside Road and the George family home on Chaussée Road.

The upper middle class colonial British rulers built many houses up on the Morne to catch the breeze and there are several grand buildings still standing. **Government House** is the nearest thing to Victorian architecture in St Lucia, rebuilt at the end of the 19th century after a hurricane in 1817 destroyed the previous building and buried Governor Seymour and many others in its ruins.

**20th century**

Since the fire of 1948, buildings in the capital have suffered from lack of imagination and are nearly all square concrete blocks in a functional style. The only notable exception is the pyramid at Pointe Seraphine built in 1993 for the Alliance Francaise. Artistic development really took off in the 20th century and St Lucia has produced painters of international renown.

**Dunstan St Omer** was born in St Lucia in 1927 into a Catholic family and is best known for his religious paintings. He created the altarpiece for the Jacmel church near Marigot Bay, where he painted his first black Christ, and reworked Castries Cathedral in 11 weeks in 1985 prior to the Pope's visit. St Omer and his four sons have also painted other countryside churches (Monchy and Fond St Jacques) and a quarter of a mile of sea wall in Anse La Raye.

**Llewellyn Xavier** was born in Choiseul in 1945 but moved to Barbados in 1961, where he took up painting. Galleries in North America and Europe have exhibited his work and his paintings are in many permanent collections. Xavier returned to St Lucia in 1987, where he was shocked by the environmental damage. He has since campaigned vigorously for the environment through his art. The Global Council for Restoration of the Earth's Environment is a work created in 1993 from recycled materials including prints, postage stamps and seals and logos of preservation societies. It is on display at the artist's studio, Silverpoint, Mount du Cap, Cap Estate, xavierl@candw.lc, T4509155 for an appointment, but he also has galleries, see p145.

see p145

**21st century**

There is still a lot of housing development around the island and designers continue to follow traditional styles with covered balconies to beat the heat, while taking advantage of modern materials. Pressure on land means that many houses have to be built on steep hillsides, using concrete stilts to support one side of the house. Roofs are multi-coloured metal panels, replacing the old corrugated sheets of the 20th century.

The art scene, on the other hand, is lively and innovative and there is a range of outstanding artists. Artists from abroad have also been drawn to St Lucia and their works can also be found in local galleries. St Lucian artists include **Ron Savory**, Ron's Atelier and Framing Co, Vide Bouteille Industrial Park, past the roundabout at the end of the airport runway (called La Clery junction), T4524412. His rich rainforest scenes and his dancing figures are impressive and he sells collectables, souvenir art, paintings from originals to limited prints to prints.

**Sean Bonnett St Remy** paints wonderful local scenes, village scenes with nostalgic charm and accuracy, he can be contacted at Photographic Images, 42 Brazil Street. **Winston Branch** is splashy, modern abstract, and shows internationally from London to Brazil. He is currently teaching in the USA. **Chris Cox** paints St Lucian birds, such as the parrot and the nightjar. He won an award at the Arts Award ceremony in January 2000 and is now head of Planning in the Ministry of Agriculture.

Other **contemporary artists** such as Arnold Toulon, Cedric George, Chris Cox, Nancy Cole, Sophie Barnard, Alcina Nolley and Jonathon Gladding exhibit their works at the Inner Gallery, see p146. **Daniel Jean-Baptiste** makes hand-painted, limited edition, silk artwork, call T4508000 for a private studio visit. **Alcina Nolley**, an artist and teacher of art, can refer you to many artists and artisans, particularly of the Arts and Crafts Association, T4532338, nolleym@candw.lc.

# Books

**Derek Walcott**, one of the Caribbean's most renowned poets and playwrights in the English language, was born in St Lucia in 1930. He has published many collections of poems, an autobiography in verse, *Another Life*, critical works, and plays such as *Dream on Monkey Mountain* (1971). Walcott uses English poetic traditions, with a close understanding of the inner magic of the language (Robert Graves), to expose the historical and cultural facets of the Caribbean. His books are highly recommended, including his narrative poem *Omeros*, which contributed to his winning the 1992 Nobel Prize for Literature. Derek Walcott was one of the founder members of the **St Lucia Arts Guild** in 1950. With the assistance of his twin brother, the late Roderick Walcott (1930-2000), a dramatist and theatre director who was St Lucia's first Director of Culture, the Guild paved the way for St Lucia's literary works and drama which produced artists of Caribbean and international merits. Other St Lucian writers worth reading are the novelists Garth St Omer (*The Lights on the Hill*) and Earl G Long (*an MD in the USA*), and the poets Jane King-Hippolyte, Kendal Hippolyte, John Robert Lee (*Artefacts*) and Jacintha Lee, who has a book of local legends. New authors to emerge in the 21st century include Anderson Reynolds, with his novel *Death By Fire*, and Michael Aubertin (a former Director of Culture) with his period drama, *Neg Maron: Freedom Fighter*.

---

## Fiction

**Aubertin**, M, *Neg Maron: Freedom Fighter,* (2000), Caribbean Diaspora Press Inc. Partly a romance and partly a historical novel about runaway slaves in the days of the British colony, much of the research for the book was taken from the author's dissertation, Patterns of Gender Socialization. Social and racial prejudice, the abuse of women, both by men and by other women, are intertwined with war and the struggle for freedom.

**Long**, EG, *Consolation*, (1994), Longman. The fictional village, Consolation, finds its rural way of life under threat when developers move in to build a hotel. Long writes about the strains on local culture and relationships when the North American leisure industry takes over and 'progress' marches in. His other novels are *Voices from a Drum* and *Slicer*.

**Reynolds**, A, *Death by Fire*, (2001), Jako Books. Set against the backdrop of real historical events in St Lucia, slavery, colonialism and plantation agriculture, as well as the Ravine Poisson landslide and two fires in Castries, the characters drawn by the author overflow with love, lust and hate and their emotions are entangled with the struggle for survival in a young country.

**St Omer**, G, *The Lights on the Hill*, (1986), Heinemann. A novella dealing with the claustrophobia of living on a small island and the protagonist's concern with lack of fulfilment together with some telling vignettes of St Lucia's landscape and society.

## Non-fiction

**Reynolds**, A, *The Struggle for Survival*. (2003), Jako Books. Ostensibly tracing the origins and outcome of the banana farmers' strike in 1993, which led to the deaths of two men, Dr Anderson Reynolds goes beyond that event to investigate the island's history, with farmers' struggles against natural disasters, slavery, colonialism and imperialism, tracing the forces which have defined contemporary St Lucian society.

## Poetry

**Hippolyte**, K, *The Labyrinth*, (1993), The Source, Castries. This collection explores themes ranging from St Lucia's rapid modernisation to the collapse of the Grenadian Revolution.

Other collections of poetry by Kendal Hippolyte include *Island in the Sun - Side Two* (1980), *Bearings* (1986) and *Birthright* (1996).

**Walcott**, D, *Omeros*, (1990), Faber and Faber. Widely considered to be his greatest achievement and the catalyst for Derek Walcott being awarded the Nobel Prize for Literature in 1992. Other works include *Sea Grapes* (1976), *The Fortunate Traveller* (1982), *Midsummer* (1984).

---

## Travelogues

**Amis**, M, *St Lucia, in Visiting Mrs Nabokov and Other Excursions*. (1993), Cape. Martin Amis writes about his holiday on St Lucia and the tensions between St Lucians and tourists: "Although you wouldn't call them hostile, they are no more friendly than I would feel, if a stranger drove down my street in a car the size of my house." The essay is a perceptive commentary on the love-hate relationship that islands have towards tourism.

# Language

The main language in Saint Lucia is English but 75% of the population also speak a patois, Lesser Antillean Creole French, called Kwéyòl. This is a language which evolved so that African slaves could communicate with their French masters and it has survived even though St Lucia has been British since 1814. It is similar to the Creole spoken in Haiti, Guadeloupe, Martinique and other former French colonies, but it is closest to the Kwéyòl of Dominica, another French island which became British. It is said that Dominicans and St Lucians understand each other 98% of the time. Standard French, however, is understood by no more than one in ten St Lucians. Kwéyòl is a formal language, with grammar and syntax, but it has only recently been written down and many Kwéyòl speakers can not in fact read it. For this reason it is successful on the radio and politicians even give speeches in Kwéyòl, particularly since it has become an official language of parliament alongside English. It has a reputation of being spoken by farmers, and the first radio programmes in Kwéyòl were broadcast early in the morning before they left for the fields, but it is spoken by St Lucians in all walks of life, including doctors, bankers, ministers and the Governor General, Dame Pearlette Louisy, who has done a great deal to promote it as a written language.

Spelling in Kwéyòl has been made fairly uniform so that all Creole/patois-speaking places are alike... not just Martinique, Dominica and Haiti in the Caribbean, for example, but other places like Mauritius. For people interested in learning a few phrases of Kwéyòl (Creole), there is a booklet, *Visitor's Guide to St Lucia Patois*, EC$14, and the *Kwéyòl Dictionary*, EC$10, available in **Valmont's Book Salon** on the corner of Jeremie and Laborie streets, and at **Sunshine Books** in Gablewoods Mall and Rodney Bay and other outlets.

For the more ambitious reader there are traditional story booklets which explain a lot about country life. Short stories are written in a style a child can understand with an English translation at the back. Examples are *Mwen Vin Wakonte Sa Ba'w* (I am going to explain it to you), which has a tale for every letter of the alphabet about an animal, or *Se'kon Sa I Fèt* (Know how it is done), a book about farm life. These books, part of a series of eight aimed at a St Lucian readership, are not available in shops (but there are other children's books in Kwéyòl which are). Contact the Summer Institute of Linguistics, Box 321, Vieux Fort, price around EC$5 each. For the serious student Jones Mondesir's *Dictionary of St Lucian Creole* (1992) would be the definitive work but it costs upwards of EC$300.

The Folk Research Centre (PO Box 514, Mount Pleasant, Castries, T4522279, F4517444,( *open Monday-Friday 0830-1630*), preserves and documents the local culture and folklore and has published several books, a cassette (EC$30) and CD (EC$60): *Musical Traditions of St Lucia. A Handbook for Writing Creole* gives the main points and features, while a *Dictionary of St Lucian Creole* and *Annou Di-Y an Kwéyòl*, a collection of folk tales and expressions in Creole and English, accompany it well. In 1999 the *New Testament* was published in Kwéyòl.

A visit to the market in Castries is one of the easiest ways for a visitor to listen to Kwéyòl being spoken by the man or woman in the street and on the next page are just a few useful phrases.

# Glossary

*Sent Lisi*  Saint Lucia
*Mwen ka apwonn Kwéyòl*  I'm learning Kwéyòl
*Mwen konnèt an ti miyèt Kwéyòl*  I know a little Kwéyòl
*Bonjou*  Good day
*Bonnapwémidi*  Good afternoon
*Souplé*  Please
*Mèsi*  Thank you
*Non mèsi*  No thanks
*Konmen pou sa?*  How much is this?
*Mwen vlé achté chimiz la*  I would like to buy this T-shirt
*Sala twò chè*  That's too expensive
*Ki sa*  What is this?
*Koté bank la?*  Where is the bank?
*Dédé*  Goodbye

# Index

# Credits

## Footprint credits

Editorial and production: Rachel Fielding, Laura Dixon, Jo Morgan
Map editor: Sarah Sorensen
Publisher: Patrick Dawson
Series created by: Rachel Fielding
Cartography: Claire Benison, Kevin Feeney, Robert Lunn,

Design: Mytton Williams
Maps Footprint Handbooks Ltd

## Photography credits

Front cover: the Pitons, Powerstock
Inside: Alamy, St Lucia Tourist Board
Cut-out images: Alamy, Powerstock
Generic images: John Matchett
Back cover: Friday night barbecue, St Lucia Tourist Board

## Print

Manufactured in Italy by LegoPrint
Pulp from sustainable forests.

## Footprint feedback

We try as hard as we can to make each Footprint guide as up to date as possible but, of course, things always change. If you want to let us know about your experiences – good, bad or ugly – then don't delay, go to www.footprintbooks.com and send in your comments.

## Publishing information

Footprint St Lucia
1st edition
Text and maps © Footprint Handbooks Ltd October 2004

ISBN 1 904777 18 X
CIP DATA: a catalogue record for this book is available from the British Library

Published by Footprint Handbooks
6 Riverside Court
Lower Bristol Road
Bath, BA2 3DZ, UK
T +44 (0)1225 469141
F +44 (0)1225 469461
E discover@footprintbooks.com
W www.footprintbooks.com

Distributed in the USA by Publishers Group West

# Complete title list

(P) denotes pocket
Handbook

# NICK TROUBETZKOY'S
## ANSE CHASTANET RESORT
### ST. LUCIA

Anse Chastanet is one of the Caribbean's most romantic hideaway resorts, nestled harmoniously amidst 600 tranquil, tropical acres with two soft sand beaches, pristine coral reefs just offshore and with some of the most spectacular views St Lucia can offer.

Enjoy 49 individually designed rooms decorated with original art in hillside or beachside setting. Resort facilities include 2 restaurants/bars, full service spa, professional scuba centre, mountain bike facility with 12 miles of dedicated private trails, boutiques, art gallery, tennis, watersports and excursions desk.

**TRANQUILITY, ROMANCE AND ADVENTURE
AT ANSE CHASTANET**

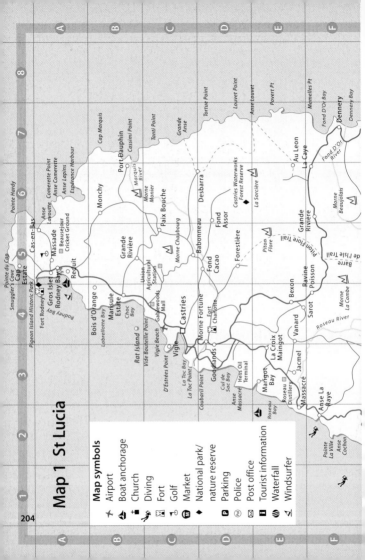

# Map 1 St Lucia

204

## Map symbols

| | |
|---|---|
| ✈ | Airport |
| ⚓ | Boat anchorage |
| ⛪ | Church |
| 🤿 | Diving |
| 🏰 | Fort |
| ⛳ | Golf |
| ◆ | Market |
| | National park/ nature reserve |
| P | Parking |
| ⓟ | Police |
| ✉ | Post office |
| ⓘ | Tourist information |
| ✷ | Waterfall |
| ✧ | Windsurfer |

Pointe du Cap
Smuggler's Cove
Pointe Hardy
Cap Estate
Cas-en-Bas
Anse Lavoutte
Comerette Point
Anse Comerette
Anse Lapins
Esperance Harbour
Fort Rodney
Pigeon Island Historic Park
Gros Isle
Rodney Bay
Reduit
Massade
Beausejour
Beausejour Cricket Ground
Cap Marquis
Monchy
Port-Bauphin
Cassimi Point
Tanti Point
Tortue Point
Louvet Point
Anse Louvet
Povert Pt
Mamelles Pt
Fond D'Or Bay
Dennery
Dennery Bay
Marquis River
Morne Monier
Desbarra
Au Leon
La Caye
Fond D'Or River
Bois d'Orange
Marisule Estate
Choc Bay
Gablewoods Mall
Labrellotte Bay
Rat Island
Vide Bouteille Point
Vigie Beach
Vigie
Paix Bouche
Grande Rivière
Union Agricultural Station
Morne Chabourg
Fond Assor
Babonneau
Fond Cacao
Forestière
Castries Waterworks Forest Reserve
La Sorcière
Grande Anse
Grande Rivière
Morne Beaujolais
Castries
Morne Fortune
Fort Charlotte
Piton Flore
Piton Flore Trail
Barre de l'Isle Trail
D'Estrees Point
La Toc Bay
La Toc Point
Coubaril Point
Cul de Sac Bay
Anse Massacre
Hess Oil Terminal
Goodlands
Bexon
Ravine Poisson
Vanard
Sarot
Morne La Combe
Roseau River
La Croix Maingot
Jacmel
Marigot Bay
Roseau Distillery
Roseau Bay
Massacré
Anse La Raye
Pointe La Ville
Anse Cochon

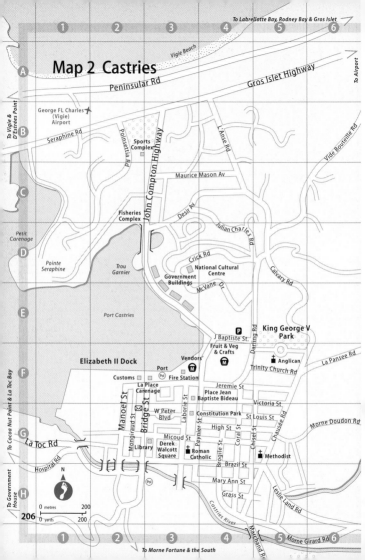

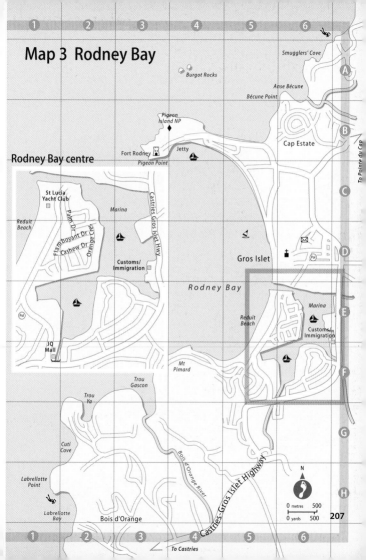

# Map 3 Rodney Bay

Smugglers' Cove

Burgot Rocks

Anse Bécune

Bécune Point

Pigeon Island NP

Cap Estate

Fort Rodney

Jetty

Pigeon Point

## Rodney Bay centre

St Lucia Yacht Club

Marina

Palm Dr

Flamboyant Dr

Cashew Dr

Orange Dr

Reduit Beach

Customs/ Immigration

Gros Islet

Pol

Rodney Bay

Marina

Reduit Beach

Customs/ Immigration

Pol

JQ Mall

Mt Pimard

Trou Gascon

Trou Ya

Cuti Cove

Bois d'Orange River

Labrellotte Point

Labrellotte Bay

Bois d'Orange

Castries-Gros Islet Highway

To Castries

N

0 metres 500
0 yards 500

**207**

# For a different view…
## choose a Footprint

Over 100 Footprint travel guides
Covering more than 150 of the world's most exciting
countries and cities in Latin America, the Caribbean, Africa, Indian
sub-continent, Australasia, North America, Southeast Asia, the
Middle East and Europe.

Discover so much more…
The finest writers. In-depth knowledge. Entertaining and accessible.
Critical restaurant and hotels reviews. Lively descriptions of all the
attractions. Get away from the crowds.